Walking Toward Your Fear

Dedicated
to Those Doctors
who have saved
my life many times
and who have helped
make living more meaningful

Dr. Bobby Brown
Cardiologist, Fort Worth, Texas

Dr. DeWitt Claunch
Family Doctor, Fort Worth, Texas

Dr. Denton Cooley
Heart Surgeon, Houston, Texas

Dr. John Fershtand
Internist with Heart Specialty, Ft. Worth, Texas

Dr. Robert Leachman
Cardiologist, Houston, Texas

Dr. Louis Leatherman
Cardiologist, Houston, Texas

H. C. BROWN, Jr.

WALKING TOWARD YOUR FEAR

✳ **BROADMAN PRESS**
NASHVILLE, TENNESSEE

© Copyright 1972 · Broadman Press
All rights reserved
4252–15
ISBN: 0–8054–5215–x

Library of Congress Catalog Card Number: 72–86333
Dewey Decimal Classification: B
Printed in the United States of America

PREFACE

In 1921, when H. C. Brown was born, we were still engulfed in the frightful streptococcal epidemic of rheumatic fever and rheumatic heart disease which involved not only the valves of the heart but the heart muscle itself. It was still often fatal in childhood, as it was for my younger sister. She died at the age of twelve after repeated attacks of rheumatic fever in the early years of the twentieth century. This was a devastating tragedy to our whole family and one of the reasons for my deciding to study medicine.

Fortunately, a good many children recovered, though most of them had damaged hearts. A few recovered entirely and are still in good health; among them are friends and patients of mine who had their acute rheumatism before the days of penicillin, which was introduced as a great lifesaver some twenty-eight years ago. Now acute rheumatic fever has become in many parts of the world, including the United States of America, a relatively rare disease following our control of the hemolytic streptococcus. This is, of course, one of the great miracles of this century.

When Mr. Brown was born, we were struggling to rehabilitate children and young adults with crippled rheumatic hearts so that they could resume school or be trained for sheltered work after months of convalescence in hospitals and at home. It was *the* great challenge of the day, and I was in the thick of it. Coronary heart disease and heart attacks were still at that time relatively uncommon.

It was in the midst of all these developments in 1921 that Mr. Brown was born. Ten years later he was one of many thousands who were felled by the prevailing streptococcus. This resulted in damage to his heart from which he suffered more mentally than physically throughout his boyhood and in later years. Finally he was released from his bondage of fear by his own spiritual rehabilitation and rescued from his physical invalidism and impending death by expert surgery. He recounts his struggling with his fears in chapter after chapter in intimate detail: his fears of the shame of his disease, of unwanted sympathy, of inability to become an athlete, of publicity, and of death itself.

I am sure that many others who have had much the same difficulties will be interested in the way these problems affected him and his lifelong struggle to overcome them. Although this is a very individual story indeed and no one has had exactly the same experiences, any individual who is as dedicated as Mr. Brown can usefully serve "the common good." The same is true of the physicians who made it possible for him to live to tell about his walking to wisdom in conquering his fear.

PAUL DUDLEY WHITE, M.D.

Boston, Massachusetts
February, 1972

FOREWORD

"Sapimus animo, fruimus anima; sine animo anima est debilis." "We think with mind, enjoy with the heart; without the mind the heart is weak."

This Latin quotation still expresses well an observation made centuries ago that the mind rules the heart. Several years ago cardiac surgeons, theologians, and religious groups discussed whether the heart was indeed a privileged organ in the body or only a servant to the mind. The mind and the heart have for ages been rivals as the center deemed responsible for courage, fear, love, hate, and even thought. The Romans must have pondered this deeply, since the Latin word for mind, *animus,* is almost identical with the word *anima* for heart.

Renewed attention evolved from the heart transplant era with the objective and logical thoughts people began to associate with the meaning of life. The mind actually *is* life. This tangible part of our being unquestionably resides in the brain, but the brain is not the mind; it is another complex anatomical organ. The mind, the being, the spirit, and the soul are perhaps the same and the master; and every other part or organ of the body is only servant to the master. One's life is spent nourishing the mind—he attempts to protect and prolong the health of the various organs or servants for optimum support of the master.

WALKING TOWARD YOUR FEAR concerns a man who for over thirty years struggled with a weak heart and tells how he triumphed over his cardiac ailment to the ultimate enrichment of his life.

"Dr. Henry Clifton Brown, Jr., 46-year-old Baptist professor of preaching, was admitted to the Texas Heart Institute (St. Luke's Episcopal Hospital), Houston, Texas, in May, 1968, with combined mitral aortic valve incompetence with unstable cardiac compensation. Cardiac catheterization revealed left ventricular failure and pulmonary hypertension resulting from valvular disease. Surgery was performed replacing the mitral valve with a discoid prosthesis and the aortic valve with a ball valve prosthesis. Cardiopulmonary bypass time using the artificial heart lung was one hour and eleven minutes. Dr. Brown recovered rapidly and was dismissed from the hospital ten days following operation on routine medications."

This is the brief hospital summary of a Dr. Brown who underwent "routine" heart surgery almost four years ago. What the record, no matter how voluminous or detailed, could not show was the enormous emotional and psychological effect the event had upon this man, a "cardiac cripple" who overcame his fear and conquered his old enemy—rheumatic heart disease.

The book Dr. Brown has written, demonstrating almost total recall of events, names, and words, and a keen insight, provided an inspiring revelation to me as a cardiac surgeon, as it showed the mental anguish and concern that a patient must endure awaiting and then experiencing major heart surgery.

The narrative account of Dr. Brown's life with rheumatic heart disease fills one with empathy for the child afflicted by a chronic devastating illness. Even today treatment is only partially effective and depends largely upon rest and confinement in bed. How many thousands of young people have been imprisoned by rheumatic fever and painful joints at the most active time of life! When the acute phase of the disease subsides, many are left with scars in the heart which persist throughout life and lead to premature death. An aphorism states that rheumatic fever "licks the joints and bites the heart," since chronic joint disease rarely occurs. In Dr. Brown's case the mitral and aortic valves were severely bitten. Confined to bed for a prolonged period like many patients, Dr. Brown benefited from that period of solitude. He had time for the contemplation and introspection that influenced his entire life and served as a powerful intellectual, spiritual, and emotional stimulus which accounted for his victory over personal adversity.

The episodes he describes when as a young boy he could not engage in the more strenuous athletic activities of his friends filled me with nostalgia. Any youngster who ever played "shinny" on roller skates will never forget the thrill he experienced while making a goalward dash with the crumpled tin can in his possession while his opponents flailed away at the "puck," his skates, and pretibial zones (shins). Each bruise was a badge of honor. But the time when the football coach implied that young Brown was a coward for not trying out for the school team was a moment of pathos which touched me almost to tears.

His love of athletics paralleled my own, and I believe helped prepare him for life. When asked about the influence of athletics upon my own life, I can relate the usual things about the spirit of competition, the joy of winning, learning endurance, self-discipline, sportsmanship, and fair play. But most important was learning how to accept adversity and defeat, and even, more important, to rise and try again and again. On the playing field young people experience the disappointment of losing but should never learn to like it. Dr. Brown refused to accept defeat and was subsequently victorious in his most important contest of life.

Everyone facing heart or any other major surgery should profit from Dr. Brown's book, for it will fill them with courage and self-confidence. Even surgeons, myself included, often accused of being aloof and cool with patients and lacking the human touch and compassion for another human being, will gain from Dr. Brown's words. Our professional life is not an easy one; we must stand our own fears and defeats without overly reacting, since it may compromise our ability to give our best to the next patient. Many times I have wanted to weep along with a bereaved family, and occasionally have wept openly. But in my profession we must concern ourselves primarily with the actual medical requirements and seek the clergy to tend the spiritual needs of the patients. We lean heavily upon the chaplaincy in our hospital. When Reverend Floyd, one of the hospital chaplains, consoled Dr. Brown, one can understand that even the clergy need occasional spiritual support, just as the surgeon must occasionally submit to another surgeon's scalpel.

When Dr. Brown recovered from his operation, he joined an organization, actually more of a fraternity, known as the Mended Hearts. This is composed of individuals throughout the world who have undergone heart surgery, and whose sole purpose is service. Their motto, "It's great to be alive and to help others," is beautiful and inspiring. Dr. Brown understands the deep meaning of that motto. He has shared his experience with others in a style that is descriptive, amusing, vivid, and touching.

DENTON A. COOLEY, M.D.

Houston, Texas
January, 1972

Contents

INTRODUCTION
FOUNDATION FOR FEAR

A young medical doctor—the senior resident intern—at Harris Hospital in Fort Worth, Texas, walked into my room. It was September, 1955.

"Hi," he said.

"Good morning," I replied.

"I guess you know that you will be going home soon. You're a very lucky man. I suppose you've been told that?" he asked.

"Yes," I answered. "Dr. Fershtand and Dr. Claunch have explained to me that I am well. It's just a matter of checking and double-checking before I am released."

I was nearing the end of my third hospital stay during the past six months. Because of modern miracle medicines and the personal concern and skills of my physicians, Dr. John Fershtand (heart specialist) and Dr. DeWitt Claunch (family doctor), I was about to be sent home as "cured" of subacute bacterial endocarditis. This dreadful-sounding disease had been 100-percent fatal before the discovery of sulfa and penicillin. I was lucky to have lived long enough after my childhood rheumatic fever for these life-saving medicines to be discovered. Apart from skilled doctors and miracle medicines, I would have died that summer of 1955.

The senior resident continued, "I need your help. Part of my responsibility in this hospital is to discover interesting cases and work up the information on the patient, the disease, and the treatment."

My heart leaped in fear! I foresaw where he was going.

"What do you do with the information?" I asked.

"This can be done only with your permission," he said. "If you allow me to use you and your illness, I would like to present your case to our medical study meeting."

"No!" I blurted out. "Absolutely not!"

Quietly he went on explaining. "Your doctors are agreeable, but they said I had to clear the matter with you."

My heart was racing with fear. My heartbeat must have leaped to 140–150 beats a minute.

I said violently, "I don't care if the doctors did say it was all right with them. It is not all right with me. I don't want you to use me as a guinea pig."

"You will not be present," the young resident explained. "We can even use a substitute name or call you Patient X or something like that, if that will help your feelings."

"No. Absolutely not," I protested.

"Why?" he asked. "Why don't you wish to allow me to tell our doctors about your case? You have had a marvelous recovery. Your case can teach other doctors how to save lives. Don't you want to help inform doctors so that they can save their patients when they get subacute bacterial endocarditis?"

This question stunned me. I had not realized what was involved. I said, "Look! I would like to help other people get well, but I can't allow you to use me as an example."

"Why?" he asked again.

"Well, Doctor, you see, only a few people know the real nature of my illness. And I want to keep it that way. If you use me in an open group meeting, the information about me will get out. I just can't do it. No. I just can't do it."

He made one more effort to persuade me. "Let me try this approach. I will guarantee that no doctor there will know who you are. I will even use numbers or letters to designate Dr. Claunch and Dr. Fershtand. I will ask them not to identify you as the patient or themselves as the doctors. In this way no one but your doctors and me can know who the patient is or who the doctors are. You may help save someone's life if you will do this."

I thought deeply. My mind raced as my heart pounded away. I dreaded for anyone to know just how sick I had been. I did not want anyone to know that I had had a heart problem all of my life, or that this disease had done additional damage to my heart.

So, again, I said, "No. I am not interested."

He looked at me for a few seconds, sadly shook his head, and walked slowly out of my room.

My conscience hurt me badly. I had a horrible day! That night I tried to justify my conduct to Dr. Claunch, who had been my personal physician since 1949.

He said, "Dr. Brown, you have only to satisfy yourself. This is the way you are. If you do not wish to have your case discussed openly, you have this privilege."

I hated the way I was. And I would have given anything in the world to have had the courage to comply with that request. But I could not. Fear paralyzed me then about my heart, just as it had done since 1931. When I was ten years old, I had had rheumatic fever with resulting damage to the aortic and mitral valves of my heart. Since then I had practiced hiding the truth about my heart problems.

When a large stone is cast into a small lake, the waves and ripples spread until they touch all shores. This serious illness I had as a child had sent ripples of fear down through the years of my life, and they had affected every place they touched.

I had a deathly fear of being known as a partial cardiac cripple.

Nothing else in my life has ever come so close to affecting me deeply. This fear hurt me every day of my life from the summer of 1931 until the morning of February 8, 1968. On that day I won a marvelous victory over a life-time fear.

For most of my life I lived as if I had a heavy weight tied around my neck. It was like driving an automobile with the brakes locked. At times I felt as if both my hands were handcuffed behind my back and both my feet were hobbled. It was, in many ways, a miserable existence. The fear of being known as a partial cardiac cripple brought frustration and despair on me for literally thousands of days.

Eventually I whipped this fear. Through the grace of God, the love and care of family and friends, and the superb care of medical doctors, I broke out of my bondage of fear. The joy of release and the pleasure of a new-found freedom have compelled me, in this book, to tell you my story.

A friend of mine has a unique philosophy for attacking fears. As befitting a wise man, he has taught his daughter to live by his philosophy. He has lived by the thesis that "the way to defeat your fear is to walk toward it." This is what he taught his daughter to do.

One night this young lady saved her life, and perhaps

the lives of her parents, by "walking toward" a fear. She had been out on a date and returned after midnight, when her parents had already retired. Shortly after she got into bed, she thought she heard a noise in her walk-in closet. Normally she would have listened a moment—with apprehension and fear—and then gone to sleep. But she said to herself, "Daddy taught me to walk toward my fears. So I will calm myself by looking in the closet."

She got up, turned on the light, and opened the closet door.

Immediately she screamed. A strange young man was standing in her closet.

He bolted past her, knocking her down, and ran down the hall.

Her father, hearing his daughter scream, bounded out into the hall in time to see a husky man in his twenties run from his daughter's room. The father ran at the intruder and tackled him, but could not hold him. The unwelcome visitor broke loose, threw open a second-floor window, and jumped to the ground. He fled before the father could get to the ground floor.

Fortunately, no one was injured, but the family were considerably shaken. They called the police, but the officers were not able to find any clues to the identity of the stranger.

My friend, telling me this story, concluded by saying, "The fact that I taught my daughter to walk toward her fear saved her life. In fact, she probably saved all of our lives!"

From this harrowing incident I have found the title for this book: WALKING TOWARD YOUR FEAR.

For most of my life, I did everything but "walk toward" my fear of being known as a partial cardiac cripple.

I tried
    denying the facts,
    hiding the truth,
    ignoring the problem,
    lying when questioned,
    worrying about details,
    brooding when upset,
    imagining wild answers,
    working out my own conclusions,
    using newspaper articles as diagnoses,
    and, in general,
    living in fear, ignorance, superstition, and anxiety.

Of course, none of these tactics aided me in the slightest in overcoming this severe problem of fear. But eventually I did learn to overcome and win!

In one sense of the word, I have had a rich, rewarding life. I had
    loving parents;
    a loving sister whom I greatly admire;
    countless lifetime friends and relatives, in Bossier
        City, Louisiana;
    four creative jobs which aided my preparation for the
        Christian ministry;
    a happy, honor-filled college career;
    a stimulating period in Kentucky as a seminary stu-
        dent and rural church pastor;
    twenty-three full, challenging, creative, and, I feel,
        successful years of teaching six thousand young
        ministers at Southwestern Baptist Theological
        Seminary;
    a wonderful marriage to Dorothy Ruth Ware, and the
        birth of two children;
    the discovery of much about God's grace and the love

of friends through the deaths of my son, Scott, and
my first wife, Dorothy Ruth;

a twenty-one-year-old daughter, Kay, whom I love
deeply, pray for daily, and who I believe will serve
God and man in some creative way;

the opportunity to edit, contribute to, or write nearly
thirty books, as well as scores of articles;

thousands of friends—of both sexes and all races—in
hundreds of cities around the world;

and a new marriage to Velma Lynn Darbo, which is
happy, creative, and satisfying in all ways.

Even though weighted down by heart fears, I have car-
ried on to the best of my ability. The thing which eats on
me at times is the question of just how useful my life could
have been, for God and man, if I had not had these acute
fears about cardiac problems. There is no way to answer
this self-probing question. And if I had not had these cardiac fears, there probably would have been other fears and
problems.

All men—all of us—know fears and problems. To fear
is to be human.

*The real issue is not what we would do without fears;
the real issue is what we do with them. Second to the real
issue is what we can do to get rid of those fears which
handicap us. And finally, what can we do for man and
God after we secure liberation from our worst fears?*

This book is all about the dimensions of the last paragraph. I tell my story to assist you in your struggle with
your fears.

This is not a medical book or even a Red Cross first-aid
brochure. It is not a magic charm. Magical cures are not
promised for the fears of your life. However, I do not rule
out sudden, dramatic turns of life which will help you to

achieve a breakout from the bondage of fear. God, your mind, your faith, and your will to win can do astonishing things. May it be so with you!

Such sudden victories usually come at the end of a long process of self-examination. This volume offers you a mirror into which you can look and look until insight comes. And this insight can bring liberation!

I will attempt in chapters 1 through 6 to take you on a journey with me as I learned at long last how to walk toward my fear. It is my prayer that you will see in my journey a way to win—a road for yourself to travel.

The last chapter of the book will pull together conclusions which I have reached after thirty-seven years of struggle. In these conclusions I pray that you will find some ideas which will help you to win your fight with your particular fear.

My purpose in this book is that you will win for yourself the same kind of victory over your fear which I won over the paralyzing fear of being known as a partial cardiac cripple.

I believe that I can help you, and I pray that you will allow me to try.

Come join me in a quest to conquer fears—especially your worst one!

Bring yourself to this quest and come with me as we go through moments of sadness, sickness, and sorrows, as well as moments of hope, happiness, and health.

You can conquer your worst fear!

I know. I have whipped one demonic fear which was thirty-seven years old.

Allow me to tell you about that victory.

Then, my friend, I believe that you can whip your worst fear!

Chapter I
WALKING WITH HOPE—
A PREVIEW

He swept into the room more than an hour early! At 6:45 P.M., Dr. Denton Cooley—surrounded by his staff and students—appeared in my room at St. Luke's Hospital in Houston, Texas.

Earlier that Sunday afternoon (May 19, 1968), two of Dr. Cooley's young team members—Drs. Arbegast and Painter—had examined me for possible surgery. They had told me they would be back about 8 P.M. with Dr. Cooley.

During the afternoon visit the young surgeons had in hand my medical report from Fort Worth, and I gave them an oral history of my condition. I had had rheumatic fever when I was ten and had lived with double heart valve damage since. In 1955 I had subacute bacterial endocarditis, which did additional damage to my heart. In February and April, 1968, I had had two severe attacks of acute congestive heart failure. At forty-six years of age, I desperately needed open-heart surgery. Without surgery I could live only thirty to sixty days longer.

Over the years I had developed the practice of telling as little as possible about my heart condition. Only a few friends knew that I had lived since my childhood with the threat of an early death hanging over me.

One doctor in 1941—when I was twenty—told me that I would be a heart invalid when I was thirty and dead when I was thirty-five. I did not fully believe him, but his stern prediction had hung over my head like a storm cloud through the years.

One result of such an opinion was to drive inward any desire I might have had to discuss my heart problem openly. Most problems worsen when pressed inward rather than expressed openly to some trusted doctor, friend, or counselor.

For some reason, which I never fully understood, I was ashamed of my health problem. I had had no direct control over the diseases which had damaged my heart; yet I was ashamed of my condition.

One reason (which I have thought may be the answer) could have been that I had always wanted to be an outstanding athlete. My heart condition denied me the opportunity to find out if I could have been. At times I bitterly resented my condition.

When I awoke on February 8, 1968, with acute heart failure, I could hardly breathe. To keep from awakening my wife, I went to the den to try to breathe. While trying to take deep breaths, I became aware that something was happening to my heart.

All of a sudden I had an impulse to laugh. It dawned on me that although I had hidden my heart condition from 1931 until that day, now all my friends would know. I had to get medical help quickly, and I realized that everyone would know that I had a serious heart problem.

This was a moment of liberation for me. I could no longer hide behind a veil of secrecy about my health;

realizing this, I felt a sense of relief.

I did not know then how dangerously ill I was. Later the doctors told me how critical had been my condition. I was at the point of death for many hours, but I finally rallied and began to improve. Dr. Claunch later told me that my total commitment to treatment helped to save my life. My attitude of relaxation, release from my old secrecy, and confidence that all would be well helped to see me through.

I cannot praise Dr. Fershtand and Dr. Claunch enough. These two highly skilled men had saved my life several times in 1955 when I had subacute bacterial endocarditis. Now they joined hands with God, six or seven dedicated, hard-working nurses in the cardiac unit at Harris Hospital, some miracle medicine and machines, and the resources of the human body to save my life again.

After spending sixteen days in the hospital, I went home and began a period of recovery. However, on April 28, I suffered a second spell of heart failure and returned to Harris Hospital. After I started to make progress, Dr. Fershtand decided that I needed immediate heart surgery. He told me that I faced three choices: (1) death from cardiac disease in two months *or less;* (2) a life as a cardiac invalid; (3) immediate heart surgery. When these three alternatives were held out to me, I immediately chose heart surgery.

I asked Dr. Fershtand for a recommendation as to a heart surgeon. He said, "You can secure anyone you want or know about. They have excellent heart surgeons in Fort Worth and Houston. The men with the most experience are those in Houston; they have performed thousands of open-heart operations and with great success."

I said, "I have heard much about Dr. Denton Cooley.

Can you recommend him?"

"Absolutely," he replied. "I can recommend Dr. Cooley, Dr. DeBakey, or any of their key associates."

"If you had to send a brother or if you had to face open-heart surgery, could you trust Dr. Denton Cooley?"

"Yes," he replied with calm confidence.

"I would like for you to get Dr. Denton Cooley for me," I replied immediately.

During this time in May, 1968, Dr. Cooley was performing his first three heart transplants, and other heart patients were temporarily being turned away at St. Luke's Hospital. For one week Dr. Fershtand tried to get a firm date for my admission to St. Luke's. Finally he succeeded.

However, it was necessary for me to wait until May 19 before I could enter the Houston hospital. After this date was confirmed, I was allowed to go home on May 8 and was ordered to do as little as possible. This period of eleven days involved some tension and anxiety lest I suffer a third and fatal heart failure before I could have "life-saving" surgery!

Finally May 19 came!

At 6:45 P.M. that Sunday evening, Dr. Painter came into the room and said, "Dr. Brown, meet Dr. Cooley."

And he came in to discuss with me my condition. I had been told by doctors in Fort Worth that I would like Dr. Cooley. "Like" cannot describe my impressions! I was fascinated by him. Standing six feet four inches tall, trim as an athlete, and handsome as a movie idol, Dr. Cooley immediately commanded my total attention by his striking presence.

Dr. Painter said to Dr. Cooley, "Dr. Brown had S.B.E. in 1958."

I asked if by S.B.E. he meant subacute bacterial endocarditis.

"Yes," he replied.

"I'm sorry, Dr. Painter, but the date was 1955." I did not know whether or not the date mattered, but I did not want to take a chance with something as important as open-heart surgery, especially since it was *my heart!* Dr. Cooley laughed heartily.

"Dr. Brown," he said, "We never make mistakes here—spelled *missteaks!*"

The room was filled with hearty laughter, and I enjoyed the warmth of this man very much.

Chaplain Ray Floyd, an Episcopal minister assigned to St. Luke's Hospital, had told my wife that Dr. Cooley had been an outstanding basketball player at the University of Texas in 1939, 1940, 1941. Since I am a lifelong sports fan, this bit of information pleased me greatly. So I asked the doctor that evening, "Are you the same Denton Cooley who was the brilliant basketball player at the University of Texas in 1939, 1940, 1941?"

He grinned at me—he was just leaning over me to examine my heart—then straightened up and turned around to look at his staff and students. When he did, they *all* bowed to him as if he were King of the Realm—and he really was King at St. Luke's.

He raised one arm high in the air and said with a big smile, "Gentlemen, how does a *modest man* answer a question like that?"

Again the room was filled with hearty laughter! If anyone had told me that I could actually enjoy getting ready for "life-saving" surgery, I would have questioned his sanity. Here I was with about thirty days or so to live unless Dr. Cooley could save me. Yet I was jesting with this brilliant and world-famous doctor and enjoying the occasion tremendously.

Dr. Cooley quickly decided to have a heart catherization done the next morning and to operate on Tuesday if
those studies were favorable.

After the surgeon left, Dr. Robert Leachman—the chief
cardiologist who would declare for or against surgery—
came to my room. He was just as warm a personality as
Dr. Cooley, and he talked with me as if he had all night
to discuss my heart problem. Upon leaving, he said, "One
final question: Do you have any anxiety about all this?"

I was not exactly sure what he was looking for, but I told
him I did, indeed, have some nervous concern about the
entire procedure. I was amazed at myself because I was
able to face my heart problems with a complete frankness
which before February 8 had been to me a total impossi-
bility.

He laughed and said, "Good! If you had said no, I would
have sent the staff psychiatrist to come examine you!"

After Dr. Leachman left, a constant stream of interns
and young medical students came by my room. They all
said something like this: "Dr. Leachman wants us to listen
to your chest. He says you have the most interesting sound
in there!"

By the time the sixth, seventh, and eighth young doctors
came in a group, I said, "Look, fellows, if you don't mind,
I'm going to charge admission and hearing fees. By doing
this, I think I can cut my bill somewhat."

Being bright, sharp young men under orders from chief
Leachman, they all replied, "That's okay with us. We will
just deduct it from your bill!" Do you know that I never
did hear any more about that plan, even though I kept
repeating my ideas up through the twelfth, thirteenth,
and fourteenth man! I guess they just forgot to notify the

bookkeeper so that he would make the proper deductions from my bill. I knew that professors could be absent-minded, but I didn't expect young heart surgeons and cardiologists to be!

The next day Dr. Leachman, Dr. Don Rochelle, and a young cardiologist from the Philippine Islands, plus two nurses, performed the heart catherization. During the three-hour examination the doctors and nurses had coffee in the examination room.

They were all so helpful that I felt free to complain. "You folks are driving me wild with that coffee. I'm a native of Louisiana, even though I have lived in Texas for nineteen years. Wherever I've lived, I have had family and friends send me Louisiana coffee, dark roast. I've not had one drop of liquid since midnight. So you are killing me with desire!"

They promised me I could have all the coffee I wanted —as soon as they were through.

That afternoon Dr. Arbegast came to say, "The studies show that you need valve surgery—probably double-valve surgery. Would you like to think it over, or have you decided what you want to do?"

I replied immediately, "I want surgery, and as soon as possible."

Dr. Arbegast said, "We can operate tomorrow, probably between noon and 2:00 P.M. Dr. Cooley will come later to confirm your decision."

Later, Dr. Cooley again swept into the room. He announced the state of my heart in his good-natured, half-humorous way. "Dr. Brown, you know you've got this old bad heart trouble, and it's not going to get any better by itself. What do you want to do about it?"

I replied, "Dr. Cooley, my doctors in Fort Worth told

me that you were the man who could fix it. I want you to fix it."

"Okay," said Dr. Cooley, "We'll fix it tomorrow. How's that?"

"That's just what I want," I said.

Dr. Cooley turned to Dr. Arbegast. "What time do you have for Dr. Brown tomorrow?"

"About noon," replied Dr. Arbegast.

"Fine," said Dr. Cooley. "I'll see you in the morning on the operating table." And away he went with a wave of the hand.

I was amazed at the calm way these talented people performed. Chaplain Floyd told me that Dr. Cooley had performed more than four thousand heart valve operations. I have read in other places that he has done more than six thousand heart operations. He performed his fourth heart transplant late the next night, after he had finished with me and several other patients. The doctors acted with calmness because they were highly competent men with a fabulous record of success. The atmosphere at St. Luke's was having a wonderfully calming effect on me.

In the mid-1950's, when heart surgery was becoming more usual, I felt that one day I would face such surgery. The prospect alarmed me. One of my seminary students who had had successful heart surgery described his experiences for me. I was so emotionally involved with the possibility of having to have such surgery that I became nauseated as he talked. I quickly broke off the conversation. In those days I viewed heart surgery as a future and remote hope but with emotions bordering on terror.

One of Dr. Cooley's anesthetists, Dr. Keats, came later on that Monday evening. Among several helpful things he said were these: "Tomorrow is a day of hope for you. A few years ago this double-valve operation could not have been performed."

About 10 P.M. a handsome young Negro orderly, a college student, came to prepare me for surgery. He looked at his order sheet and noted that I was a minister-teacher. He said, "I'll tell you, Doc, you are in the hands of the greatest surgeon in the world. He'll take care of you. And besides, we don't lose no heart patients here. I can't remember when we lost a heart patient."

This young man impressed me deeply. He was about six feet tall (perhaps 5'11"), weighed about 170 to 175 pounds, had medium-black skin, and a clean-cut, handsome face. He did not look like Muhammed Ali, but he had the same kind of clean, open face as the former heavyweight champion.

I was touched by his heart of compassion as he encouraged me to believe that all would be well. He told me that he was a premed student at Texas Southern, and that his goal in life was to become a heart surgeon and serve on the staff of Dr. Cooley. His eyes sparkled as he told me of his dreams.

By the time this young man left me at 10:30 P.M., I was beginning to believe all of these people. My former fears of being a heart patient and of having heart surgery were fast disappearing.

Nevertheless, you still have anxiety about such surgery. And you still think about dying—at least I did. I recalled the experiences of John F. Kennedy as a young senator. He faced invalidism or dangerous surgery during which he might die. He chose to face death in order to live a full life. This was also my choice.

I could go home, resign my work, and squeeze out a few

extra months by nonactivity. But I decided on surgery in the hope of having a better life. Besides, as the young orderly said, "We don't lose no patients at St. Luke's." Tomorrow was going to be a day of hope for me!

I slept lightly, but morning found me calmer than I had ever believed I could be. About 11:00 I was supposed to wash my chest with a special soap and to be given a shot in preparation for surgery. At 9:30 Dr. Cooley's nurse, liaison between the doctor and the patients' families, came to me to give me a final briefing.

As we talked, I remembered something. In Harris Hospital the nurses kidded me about the heart transplants which Dr. Cooley was then beginning. One nurse said, "What are you going to do if Dr. Cooley decides to give your heart to someone else?"

Well, the joke about this was that I needed a new heart, or at least a repaired one, myself. Besides, no one would have wanted my heart! In fact, I was rather tired of it myself—at least as it was! But I played the game and thought of my answer. I took a small yellow 5 x 8-pad and wrote on it with red ink in big bold letters these words:

DEAR DR. COOLEY:
    Just a simple valve job please!
                    H. C. BROWN, JR.

The Harris hospital nurses enjoyed this note, especially when I promised that I would paste it on my chest before surgery. Well, I didn't do that, but I did give it to Dr. Cooley's nurse. She assured me that she would give it to him and that he did, indeed, have a very warm sense of humor.

The nurses at St. Luke's, like those at Harris, had their own version of humor. At St. Luke's the nurses kidded me about being a minister-teacher. One of them, Miss Evans, started calling me "the talking doctor" the second day I was there, and she kept it up until after I left. I thought I knew what she meant, so about three days after surgery I asked her, "What do you mean, 'the talking doctor'?"

She replied quickly, "Well, you make your living by talking, and our doctors make their living by working!"

That morning of surgery, as the liaison nurse instructed me concerning what I was to do, Miss Evans came in and asked, "Well, how is our talking doctor today?"

It was as relaxed a scene as if I had encountered her at the post office and heard her say, "Well, how are you doing today?"

Her calm, professional, yet warm and sympathetic attitude made me smile at her.

About this time—10:00 A.M.—two aides arrived from surgery.

"You can't be after me," I protested. "You are two hours early." They told me that two operations had been cancelled, and they did want me next.

I hadn't washed with the sterile soap or had my shot to begin the anesthetizing process. I hadn't even had time to start getting tense! I was anxious, of course, but the night and morning had gone so well that I was amazingly relaxed when the surgery aides came. The nurse gave me a shot; and the men from surgery put a surgical gown on me, strapped me on the cart, and rolled me away to face open-heart surgery.

On Sunday and Monday, while I answered hundreds of questions from dozens of doctors, I had met a young resident intern from Brazil, Dr. Juca. He had told me that in Brazil, even though he was a Catholic, his best friend was the son of a Southern Baptist missionary couple. When he discovered that I was a Baptist minister-teacher, he seemed delighted. He made numerous visits to my room. On Tuesday morning, when the surgical aides started wheeling me down the hall, Dr. Juca came up and walked along with me. He assured me that all would go well.

When the cart stopped, I asked where we were.

He said, "You are just outside of the operating room."

I was nearly asleep, and I remember him saying as he gripped my hand firmly, "I will be praying for you." I thanked him.

I felt alone!

The last thing I remember before going out was trying to pray. It was a praying time!

Dr. Cooley and his team performed a double-valve replacement—still one of the rarest and most delicate of heart operations—and apparently it went extremely well. When I awoke around 3:00 P.M., my first thought was, "Well, at least I didn't die in surgery!" The folks at St. Luke's were right. It was a day of hope for me.

The only hard time I had was in the recovery room. Because of extremely crowded conditions at that time— now corrected by a new medical center in a twenty-seven-story tower—and a few unpleasant experiences with nurses and doctors in recovery, I was moved to a private room with private nurses on the third day.

It was good to be back in the quiet of a hospital room. I also appreciated the service of the nursing staff on my wing, as well as my private-duty nurses.

Miss Evans, Mrs. Reed, and the other third-floor nurses at St. Luke's seemed like "old pros"! (The entire third floor was devoted to heart patients.) They made not the slightest fuss or bother about the fact that I was facing heart surgery. After all, thousands of children, men, and women had had open-heart surgery at St. Luke's, next door at Methodist Hospital, and at numerous other hospitals around the world. They reflected, it seemed to me, a spirit of confidence which said, "So you have come in for heart surgery! Well, would you like to get your nails clipped while you are here?" They appeared to be totally confident that all would go well for me.

Miss Evans and Mrs. Reed in particular had cheerful attitudes at all times. I feel that sometimes good nurses get taken for granted. They never should be. They are a vital link in the "patient-hospital-staff-doctor-nurse" relationship. A serious breakdown at any point can damage an already ill man, woman, or child. As much as doctors, they need a good "bedside manner." I would guess that 90 percent or more of the ones I have encountered in my eleven trips to hospitals have been thus qualified. I am grateful for the superb service and care rendered to me by seventy-five to one hundred nurses during the last thirty-three years.

On the fourth day after surgery, I was instructed to walk. I told the private-duty nurse, a very firm person, "I'm too weak to walk!"

"Weak or not," she replied, "you are going to walk. Dr. Leachman left orders for you to walk, and you are going to walk!"

She further said in sternness and good humor, "Your wife is not here. So get out of that bed, put your arm around my neck, and I'll help you walk!"

I got up and walked! About eight feet, but I walked.

On the seventh day one of the young surgeons told me that I could go home. I think they needed the space for sick people! I told him that I doubted that I had the strength to leave yet.

Dr. Leachman, getting a report on this conversation, soon appeared in my room. He said, "I understand that someone is trying to run you off. I just came to tell you that it really is too early for you to leave. I believe that you ought to stay as long as one who has had an appendectomy."

You can guess, of course, that this calm, humorous approach to what was for me a "big problem" pleased me greatly. Matters did continue to go so well, however, that I was dismissed on the eleventh day.

At home all the old fears of being known as a heart patient had long since gone. I now discussed my experiences openly with my friends as they came to visit. Not only had I been given a "new heart," but I had been liberated from a burden and fear which had plagued me for thirty-seven years.

I returned to work eighty-eight days after open-heart double-valve surgery. I thank God each day for the opportunity and I pray regularly for Dr. Cooley and his team. I eagerly watch new developments by Dr. Cooley and his team, proudly telling all who will listen, "Those are the folks who took care of me."

If you ever need him, I can tell you the same thing the young orderly told me: "He is the greatest heart surgeon in the world, and we don't lose no patients at St. Luke's."

Whatever your fear or problem is, I can also tell you what Dr. Keats told me that night before open-heart surgery, "Tomorrow can be a day of hope for you!"

It can be.

Chapter II

WALKING IN THE DEPTH
OF THE VALLEY

I experienced acute heart failure on February 8, 1968.

And a second heart failure a few weeks later on April 28.

I had thought I was doing well between February 8 and April 28, but not so!

The fear which hits you when you can't breathe is as real the second time as the first. It carries a punch—a paralyzing punch—and it hits you where it hurts: mind, chest, stomach, and legs. You think you may be dying. And you could be!

This is a sharp, natural fear—as real as a snake at your feet, a gun in a stranger's hand, a malignancy report from your doctor, or the harsh glare of a fast-rushing car about to crash into you head-on. The fear which came with my second heart failure was as intense as the first time.

At the time of my second heart failure, I made extensive notes and wrote out word for word my impressions concerning how I felt about facing death in a matter of hours or days. (It is my habit to make notes and keep records of all significant events in my life.) Because these words were written during an acute crisis in my life, I have called this chapter "Walking in the Depth of the Valley."

It was Sunday, May 5, in Fort Worth, Texas. (These notes were written out Monday Night.) I awakened at 5:00 in my sixth-floor room at Harris Hospital, sat on the side of the bed, and took stock of my life.

That Sunday morning as I looked out a west window, the rising sun's rays were striking windows in houses, cars, and buildings and reflecting back to me warmth and courage from God's beautiful world. I wanted to get well! I wanted to live! As much as I ever have, I wanted to serve God by serving mankind for him! The scene was singularly awe-inspiring and graphically creative.

In this quiet, lovely setting I talked to the Lord for nearly one hour.

I made—as far as was in me—a complete committal of my all to God. It was time to do so. I was soon to face extensive tests to determine my true condition and fitness to face open-heart surgery.

This committal I made specifically included myself; Velma; Kay; all possessions of whatever value; all of family in Fort Worth, Texas; Bossier City, Louisiana; Alexandria, Louisiana; Kansas City, Missouri; Baton Rouge, Louisiana; and San Mateo, California; my total work at Southwestern Baptist Theological Seminary; my work of writing with my publishers; and all of my hopes, ideas, ideals, and dreams of the future. I did believe that, as serious as was my condition, I would have a future.

At this moment I felt that nothing but total commitment mattered. Neither life nor death mattered—only that I be in God's will.

This had been easy—really easy—to say—to think—to

write *before*. But I had never said it before with the total conviction I felt this time. Neither had I ever said it with the sure conviction I felt that *I could die* in surgery in a matter of days.

(At this point my impressions, as I recorded them Monday night, move from the Sunday morning worship experience to thirty-six hours later on Monday night, about 7:00. I am reproducing these thoughts as I wrote them that night.)

Thus I wrote it (those things set out above). I did not say it believing that I would die. *I believe and think that I will live. But I said it knowing that in open-heart surgery anything is possible.*

I am trying to stress: (1) the depth of my conviction and (2) the seriousness of the times—days—hours before me. Total commitment is easy to talk about in the abstract, and it is easy to talk about if you feel that you hold an *open end on time!* Most of us hope and/or assume that we have this "open end on time." But it is not so for every one!

It is *never* true for anyone. It may *only seem* to be true.

The idea of total commitment is easy to talk about even when we think or feel that we have a generous *expanse of time*. It is when time *closes down*—when some vital part gets cut off or threatened—that we come face to face with a need for total commitment to God.

This may be simply the way *man* is—we are.

I am not different from others.

So, that time (on Sunday) has helped me face the passing hours by (1) placing self, all others, and all things in proper relationship to God; and (2) by placing my personal physical existence as to its present state in proper relationship to God.

So, when all in (1) above and all in (2) above are in proper relationship to God, then *all* has to be all right. Do they not? Yes! They all do have to be all right.

These thoughts—prayers came out of an *hour* or more of praying on Sunday morning. I felt better then. That was thirty-six hours or so ago, and the feeling of security in the Lord continues now on Monday night as I write these notes. My convictions are these:

One, I feel I still hold all dear ones as belonging to God in a special way—he takes care of his own—so I can release them to him with the full assurance that all is well with all of them. *Two*, I feel a growing awareness that no matter what happens to me, I will be all right and will be in God's hand. If I should die in surgery, then I have won "the ultimate victory." And if I should survive surgery, then I have been given the right to continue as a servant *here* and *now* for God's people. And joy of joys! I will have been given that right in relationship to all my dear ones: Velma, Kay, Elizabeth (my sister), and all the family, and all my friends—God does care for his own!

Praying for these things through yesterday and now rethinking them (it is 7:23 P.M.) as I look out over Fort Worth again and record these impressions, I find that these two worship periods have all helped me.

No one but God knows what the next several days can hold, but this *I do:* "I give myself and my all to him to be used as he wills. Again, as best *I* know how, I totally commit myself, my dear ones, and my all to God!"

As the man said in Scripture, "Lord, I believe! Help thou mine unbelief (weakness)!" Amen!

I continued to pray, to believe, and to trust God. I also continued to record my impressions from Tuesday, May

7, through May 19. On May 19 I entered the hospital in Houston.

Sunday night, May 19, 1968, at St. Luke's Hospital:
I am alone in my hospital room. It is 11:00.
It is now thirty-six hours until open-heart surgery. I will lay my life down on that operating table!
I have met Denton Cooley!
And I trust him and the Lord!
Yes, I am afraid!
But I trust Denton Cooley and the Lord!

Chapter III
WALKING ON SHAKY LEGS

Fear played only a small part in my life from my birth until I was ten years old. Fear, in 1931, entered my life with vigor and force. It has been a constant companion with various degrees of domination ever since.

A Dangerous Disease

Prior to the summer of 1931, I had been energetic, active, and full of life. As far as I remember, I was, for the only time in my life, in overall excellent health. Following a throat infection in the late summer of 1931, I developed rheumatic fever. The onset of this disease—still dangerous but not feared now as much as it was prior to the full use of sulfa, penicillin, and various antibiotics—slipped silently upon me that hot summer.

Doctors think that rheumatic fever attacks people usually between the ages of five and fifteen, but that it can occur at any age.[1] Rheumatic fever accounts for almost all of the heart disease found in young children, teen-agers, and young adults. Any part of the body can be damaged by rheumatic fever; but damage to the heart, which can be for a lifetime, is the most dangerous.

Rheumatic fever attacks the heart muscle and heart valves by scarring them. When these parts of the heart are scarred, they do not function normally, and the work of the heart is impaired. The victim often has not only physical problems but problems of anxiety and tension as well.

Although some patients recover from rheumatic fever without heart damage, this disease has a history of repeating itself. As new attacks of rheumatic fever occur, the heart is likely to be damaged sooner or later; or it may be damaged more severely if it is already injured.

I have only the barest memory of that tragic sore throat which led to rheumatic fever. The first time I became aware that I was ill was on a hot August day about nine or ten o'clock in the morning. Rather than going about my usual summer day's activities with the neighborhood gang, I sat on my front porch in the shade and read the morning away.

That morning, my mother asked me why I was not playing with the other kids. I told her that I didn't want to play; besides, I had rather read. At best this was a confused answer. Even though I have loved to read for as long as I can remember, my conduct in selecting a book over neighborhood games was not exactly normal for me at the age of ten.

Several more times my mother asked about my feelings, since I did not venture out with the crowd all day long.

When my father came in from work—as a railroad switchman for the Kansas City Southern Railroad—I heard them discussing my conduct. By this time I had started to think that something was wrong. For the entire length of one bright day, I had chosen to sit, rock, and read rather than run and play.

My mother came out on the porch with a thermometer in her hand and took my temperature.

"Yes," she said to Daddy, "He's got fever!"

That fever scared Mother, as fever scared her all of her life. It spoke of some unknown illness lurking in the human body, and she always had a fearful respect for it. I don't think she ever learned to make the appraisal of fever which doctors make: Fever is the signal that a disease is present; it is not the disease itself.

For several days my mother hovered about me, checking my forehead, taking my temperature, and asking numerous questions. As I recall, I never seemed to have any specific answers. I simply stated over and over that I did not feel well, that I did not want to play, and that I wanted to sit and rock and read. Some of my lifetime older friends in Bossier City have told me that the first memory they have of me were those days when I would rock and read all day long on our front porch.

Several days after my first awareness of possible illness, my mother and father took me to our family doctor for an examination. The doctor's sure verbal probing quickly turned up the fact that quite recently I had had a severe sore throat. He checked my heart numerous times with the stethoscope and took my blood pressure. This was my first experience with these instruments which I would come to fear and hate during crises in my adult life. The doctor also X-rayed my heart.

I found these X-rays far more interesting than the stethoscope, blood pressure cuff, and mercury gauge. These latter items, then and until later years, reminded me of secret tools for delving around in my "innards"! I could have no part in the investigation. (I learned a long time ago that what I didn't know could and did hurt me because of personal anxiety.) I could only worry, becoming taut with fear that sent my pulse racing and my blood pressure rising. I could not know what was happening. But the X-ray procedures and pictures were another matter. I could see and examine the pictures. The doctor showed me what my chest looked like. He took a pointer and traced out various things in the picture he wanted me to see. I was deeply interested in the details he described.

After a number of visits, the doctor declared that I had rheumatic fever, with mitral and aortic valve damage. I had never heard of rheumatic fever, couldn't spell it for many years, and came to hate the sound of the words. Even now I have broken out in a cold sweat as I have tried to recapture these memories!

The events of the day on which the doctor told my mother, father, and me that I had rheumatic fever with heart damage made no deep impression on me. But those events have jarred me many times since. I had no emotional or physical backlog of experiences with, or information about, rheumatic fever which could frighten me. I have often been quite glad that I couldn't look forward from 1931 to the 1970's as well as I can now look back! It is in this sense that that old saying—"What you don't know can't hurt you"—is true.

The impressions which stood out in my mind about those days of medical investigation were that I had something seriously wrong, that I was to be put to bed for many long weeks—six to eight, I think it was—and that I had to be extremely careful about colds and respiratory infections.

I became aware, as the doctor talked to me, that I had something wrong which had to be lived with. I had had a streptococcal infection which resulted in scarred mitral and aortic heart valves. I had had rheumatic fever, and my life would never be the same again. And these last forty years have proved that the doctor was right.

In 1931 medicine had no so-called miracle drugs such as the sulfa family, penicillin family, and other antibiotics. Effective heart surgery was twenty-five to thirty years in the future. Rest was the primary way to fight rheumatic fever, and rest and constant care with colds must become a way of life for me.

Fear entered my life with reckless abandon in those days following the attack of rheumatic fever. I had a disease which seemed to be uncontrollable. I had come to know a private hellish fear. My life changed drastically in the long hot summer of 1931.

A Misdirected Philosophy

Our family doctor treated me according to the acceptable medical views of his day. Since he had no access to miracle drugs or surgical procedures, he ordered me to rest for a long time and to be extremely careful about colds. The ironic element in that advice was that I had only the faintest notion of *how* to avoid colds. A stern lecture filled with one, two, threes would have helped—I think. I may have gotten such a lecture, but I have no recollection of specific instructions on how to avoid colds or how to care for myself if I caught one.

The doctor lectured my parents, and my parents lectured me, about rest and being careful. I heard these words—"You must rest" and "You must be careful"—until I came to hate them.

The principles followed by our family doctor and by my parents were the accepted medical way in 1931. Decades would pass before doctors found better procedures for the care of rheumatic fever patients.

One heart doctor in New England during the 1930's led the school administration of his city to set up a special school for children who had rheumatic fever, scarlet fever, polio, and other disabling diseases. The school had specially trained teachers, special beds, and planned periods for rest. On the surface one would think that the plan would be excellent. But no. The doctors and educators discovered that they were rearing a generation of emotional cripples. They discovered that in most cases handicapped children would stop and rest as needed and that other kids would understand. The special school made those handicapped children excessively anxious about themselves. The program was eventually abandoned.

My family doctor, my parents, my teachers, and numerous adult friends engaged in a common cause of watching me and guarding me from harm. Although all of these folks acted with the best light and knowledge they had, they added a burden to the emotional and physical load I was already carrying. And frankly, I was carrying my part rather poorly, I think.

Yet it is entirely possible that all these words of caution may have saved my life. I really do not know what stupid things I might have done if I had not had this careful guidance. I will never know the full answer to this question.

I do know that this philosophy of extremely careful protection after rheumatic fever almost made a cardiac cripple out of me. It didn't always take a special school with a misdirected philosophy of protection to cripple a kid. The same crippling could be accomplished—or almost so in my case—by those people most concerned about a kid's health: his doctors, family, teachers, druggists, church leaders, and other friends, some of whom were young.

I must state in all honesty that I seldom had a clear-cut picture of my true medical condition. I am not talking only about the time when I was ten years old. For most of my life my picture of my medical and physical condition was at best cloudy and confused. *A large part of this and the total responsibility for this condition must be mine.* The conquest of some of my acute cardiac fears came *only* when I could fully accept the responsibility for my condition. I will say more later about setting myself free from acute cardiac fears.

A Slender Hope for a Full Life

Hope was a vague possibility for rheumatic fever victims as late as the 1930's and up to the 1940's. Even though Sir Alexander Fleming discovered the basic principles for unlocking the forces of penicillin around 1929, this drug did not get into widespread public health use until after World War II. Military doctors had some access to penicillin during the war; but as Dr. Fershtand, a former naval doctor, told me, "It almost took an order from the admiral to give a shot of penicillin." The reasons were that it was scarce, new, and not completely tested as to its long-range effects.

So, in the absence of medical or surgical hope in the years from about 1931 to 1951, my long-term health prospect looked dim. In fact, even carrying out simple jobs was extremely difficult for me as a young man.

During the summer of 1941, I worked briefly in a jewelry store and pawn shop and then spent about six weeks working for a feed and seed company. Even though both of these positions were modest in their demands on me, my health problems caused constant difficulties. With each new obstacle and each new problem, my anxieties about my heart increased. I did gain valuable business world experience but made no progress in walking toward my fear.

I spent about two months working in the jewelry store and pawn shop. The owner, Mr. Wall, we called him—a shortened form for Wallinsky, as I recall—was a most discerning man. He noticed that I sat down as often and for as long as I could. Stamina has been a problem with me since I was ten years old.

He asked one day, "H. C., why do you sit down so much of the time? You know that I like for my employees to stand, to be alert and ready to serve customers as soon as they walk in the store. Why do you sit so much?"

"Mr. Wall," I replied, "I have bad health problems, and I tire easily. I sit down in order to conserve strength."

"Well," he said, "I knew you had to have a reason. It is not normal for a twenty-year-old young man to spend so much time on his rear end. I tell you what I'm going to do. I'm going to put you back in the pawn shop and let you spend part of each day rechecking the accuracy of all my pawn shop records for the last five years."

So, he got me a stool and started teaching me the minor details about his business. Mr. Wall, I felt, was extremely kind and discerning. Rather than assuming I was lazy, which I was not, he got at the heart of the matter with careful questioning. I liked him for his thoughtfulness. One of the young Jewish saleswomen in the store told me, "You see, Mr. Wall wants full activity from all employees. That is his way. That is the Jewish way."

I was grateful for his personal kindness, and I was interested in his business acumen. He taught me something about how to treat people, how to ask questions instead of jumping to false conclusions, and how to be a diligent worker. All of these characteristics would serve me well in the Christian ministry.

After spending most of May and June working for Mr. Wall, I got an opportunity to be a full-time bookkeeper for a small feed and seed company. Sitting down was part of this new job. My duties involved a small amount of direct sales work, keeping an extremely small set of books, and occasionally loading a few sacks of feed and seed for private customers. I only did the latter work when the full-time warehouse man was not present.

As you can guess, loading fifty- or hundred-pound sacks posed a problem for me. I discovered that, as much as I didn't like to do so, I had to ask the customers to help me load anything over fifty pounds. The warehouse man, a friendly Negro man named Joe, taught me how to position the dolly (the piece of equipment for stacking and moving heavy sacks) right next to a stack of feed so that I could drag the top sack down onto the dolly without having to lift it. Then I could drag the sack left or right until it was arranged properly on the dolly. In this way I could move up to two hundred pounds at one time. I always asked the customers to back their cars up to our loading dock, to open the trunk, and to help me drag the sacks off the edge of the dock into the car. Since the weight was going down, and since the customer held one end and I held one end, "I" could load two to three hundred pounds of feed and seed, one sack at a time, into trunks of cars.

For a young man of twenty to have to resort to such tactics sounds silly, I know, but I cite it to point out one of the many kinds of adjustments that a cardiac patient has to make in order to hold a job. Probably the constant refrain I had heard for ten years—"take care of yourself"

—caused me to use such precautions.

In August, 1941, a friend of mine told me that the construction company building the Louisiana Ordnance Plant (a shell manufacturing and storage complex) near Minden, Louisiana, needed workers of almost all kinds. So I asked for a day off at the feed store, went to the office near Minden, and applied for work. I quickly got an approval for office work provided I could pass the physical examination. The thought of not getting this new job at $35.00 per week (my salary at the jewelry store and the feed store was $15.00 per week) because of my rheumatic heart condition put me under immediate pressure.

The physical examinations were conducted somewhat like a preliminary military physical. We male applicants stripped, stacked our clothes in a pile, held on to our wallets, and stood in line.

We stood and stood and stood. The longer I stood, the tireder I became. I desperately wanted that job, but I feared I would be rejected because of my heart damage.

For one of the few times in my life, I shared my heart fears and anxieties with those total strangers lined up with me. I had always been ashamed of my rheumatic condition and had never discussed it if I could avoid it. So, for me to talk to total strangers about the most painful matter of my life reveals the acute nature of my anxiety.

I should have learned a valuable lesson that day, but in my anxiety I did not. The men in line formed semicircle pockets for talking as we waited. When I told those men, all older and more rugged than I, about my heart problems and my fears of rejection, they were to a man sympathetic.

One man said, "You've got to relax, kid. You'll make it."

Another said, "Look, I'll get you a Coke, and I have some

aspirin in my clothes. They will help you relax." He left his place in line, got a box of aspirin out of his trousers, bought me a Coke, and patted me on the back. He also encouraged me to relax. He noted the hard thumping in my throat, caused by my damaged heart muscle and valves, and observed that unless I relaxed I would *not* get the job.

I should have noted that those older, wiser, and healthier men did not ridicule me at all. As far as I could tell, they all empathized with me, encouraged me, and predicted favorable results. This should have helped me overcome my fear to be known to be a cardiac case. I suppose, however, that because this encounter was brief and the men were strangers, the event left only a minor deposit with me.

Finally my time came. The medical doctor, a young man in his early thirties, with a two- or three-day-old beard and an unfastened tie, put the stethoscope to my chest. He listened for about ten seconds, removed his stethoscope, and said, "Rheumatic fever?"

"Yes," I replied weakly.

He did what I have seen a number of doctors do through the years. He put his stethoscope back on my chest and gave me a thorough examination. While I was standing taut and rigid, I looked at the guy behind me and he gave me an "all is OK" sign popular in those days and still used sometimes. (In this sign you put your thumb and index finger together to form the letter "O" and extend the other three fingers.) I shook my head slowly and sadly at him because I was not at all sure that all was OK.

Finally the doctor finished and said, "You don't qualify to do construction work."

"But doctor, I'm applying for office work *only!*" I said

excitedly in a high-pitched voice.

"Oh," he said. He took my papers and read them.

"So you are," he said. "Do you really need this job?"

I thought, Man, everyone in the summer of 1941 needs a job!

"Yes sir," I replied, with hope rising.

"Well, I'll approve you for office work *only*." When he said that, he pointed at my chest.

"Do you understand the seriousness of your problem?"

"Yes, sir," I said, half lying, with as much sincerity as I could.

"OK," he said again, "to do office work only." He wrote these words on my papers.

"And," he said, "promise me that you will lift nothing heavier than a typewriter—ever. OK?"

"Yes, sir," I replied eagerly.

After dressing and finishing my paper processing, I went outside. My father had brought me to the plant to apply for work. He was talking with some of the men who had been in line with me. By mere chance he had asked them if they had seen me and how much longer they thought I would need.

The men told him that they had been in line right in front of me and that I should be out any minute. Most of them had been checked out in three to four minutes as to hearts, lungs, possible hernias, and a few general questions. The doctor had taken about twelve to fifteen minutes with me.

When I came out grinning from ear to ear, all of them—about four men, as I recall—rushed up to say, "You got it, didn't you, kid?"

"Man, I got it!" I replied happily.

A Shocking Prediction

With this tension-filled start I began a year's work at the LOP—the Louisiana Ordance Plant. The plant grounds encompassed something like sixteen thousand acres. It was necessary to have widely scattered buildings for assembling and storing the military shells to be manufactured there.

Administration buildings, roads, shell assembly buildings, equipment buildings, and hundreds of concrete igloos for shell storage were to be built. As I recall, in general figures, the total plant was supposed to cost about fourteen- to fifteen-million dollars, but ended with a cost of about thirty million. In the summer of 1941, thirty-million dollars was an enormous sum of money. Thousands of people from north Louisiana, and from all over the nation, found equipment at the LOP.

About three months after I went to work in the office of the equipment division, I snagged a finger on a nail and developed a fingernail infection. Since I could not type, the equipment superintendent sent me to the infirmary to get my hand checked.

The doctor at the clinic was the same man who had admitted me for employment. He looked at the papers in his hand and said, "Brown? Brown! Don't I know you?"

"Yes," I said, "You examined me and allowed me to go to work in the equipment office."

"How are you getting along?" he asked quietly. The clinic was almost empty, and he seemed to be in a talking mood.

"Fine," I replied, "I'm still beating that typewriter and keeping our big ledger records on trucks and other equipment."

He lanced the boillike swelling around my fingernail, applied some medicine, bandaged it, and said, "Sit down. I would like to talk to you."

I sat down quietly but with considerable apprehension. I had come to hate and to fear lectures on rheumatic fever.

He said, "Do you understand the serious nature of your heart problem?"

I said with about a half truth that I thought so—at least in general.

He went on talking as if he had not heard me. Only slowly did I realize that this was to be one of the most painful hours in my life. It would shape nearly every waking moment for the next twenty-seven years.

The doctor said, "National insurance statistics show that people who have had rheumatic fever become invalids by the time they are thirty and that they are dead before thirty-five!"

I sat transfixed! Stunned!

I had had three plain-talking doctors during the years of 1931–1941, but I had never heard anything like this.

He went on at length—for about thirty minutes—quoting from insurance charts, and reading paragraphs from medical books. All the time he talked, I sat silent, still dazed. I had never realized the condition I was in. I didn't know that I would be an invalid in ten years and dead in fifteen!

He finished by saying, "I have told you all of this so that you can take care of yourself." He appeared to be genuinely interested in my well-being.

I left the clinic feeling like a zombie. I recall driving down one of those gravel roads leading to the equipment division office and repeating over and over, "My God! My God! My life is two thirds over, and I am just twenty years old. I'll be an invalid in ten years." I repeated these words over and over and over.

Back at the old farmhouse we used as an equipment office, I worked in silence for the remainder of the day. A number of fellow clerks inquired several times if I were ill. To each one I replied that I didn't feel well but that I was all right.

Of course I was lying. I was scared nearly out of my mind. I was not ready to die—even in fifteen years. At that time, as well as for all of my life, I feared to be an invalid even more than I feared dying. If I died, I knew God would take care of me with no inconvenience to him. I believed there was unlimited room in heaven. But becoming an invalid was another matter. As an invalid I would cause problems for my parents, sister, doctors, friends, and wife and children should I ever get married.

Invalidism—a horrible thought for a twenty-year-old!

Death—before thirty-five—a tragic idea for a twenty-year-old!

These were the prospects for my immediate future, according to the medical doctor!

I told no one about this bleak prediction for my life until the late 1950's. The exact date has slipped my mind, but it was some years after I had subacute bacterial endocarditis in 1955. During a visit to Dr. Fershtand, I asked him to discuss something wth me. I must have been around thirty-five to thirty-seven at the time.

The chilling prediction of that doctor in Louisiana had hardly left my conscious mind since 1941, not to mention how tenaciously it had hung in my subconscious. So I told the story of the Louisiana Ordnance Plant physician to Dr. Fershtand.

I finished by asking, "Am I really in such critical position? I have beaten the invalid-by-thirty-part, but am I in danger of imminent death?"

Without hesitation and with a voice ringing with anger, he spat out a popular expletive.

He was fully aware of my emotional hangup about people knowing me as a cardiac case. He knew about my acute anxiety when being given a heart examination. He had long ago learned to take his time in checking me and to recheck me again five or ten minutes after his first examination. Almost always the second checking would be somewhat normal as to blood pressure and heart rate. The first check would often show 180 or 190 over 100 to 120, with a pulse rate of 120 to 140. The second check would show 140 to 150 over 80 to 90, with a heart beat of 80 to 90. He had learned to give me a few minutes to relax after I discovered that I had not "fallen apart" since my last visit. As soon as I saw that he reacted calmly and naturally after checking me, I would relax.

Now he pointed out to me that since 1941 medicine had acquired a whole battery of so-called miracle drugs. Doctors were making great strides every day in heart surgery and were learning more and more about the emotional factors involved with each individual heart patient.

Then he told me something which would have spared me enormous grief if I had known it fifteen years earlier. He explained that national insurance statistics embraced tens of thousands of cases. The death rate average of thirty-five was obtained, he explained, by adding—as a clear-cut, simple illustration—the tragic death of a one-year-old baby with the more fortunate rheumatic fever victim who died at sixty-nine. So one plus sixty-nine equaled seventy, which, divided by two, equaled thirty-five. He said that this was the way one had to understand national combinations of statistical material. He further explained that general statistics said nothing at all about one individual case. Statistics could relate only to what would happen to large groups of people.

This was the first hour since I was twenty when I could see the sunshine about my health. *Dr. Fershtand planted seeds which would mature over the next decade into complete freedom from fear to be known as a cardiac case.*

A Bad Personal Reaction

Beginning in 1931, I had a real disease problem. This was not an artificial dilemna. Rheumatic fever was serious and it mattered greatly. But as bad as was my physical problem, as inept as were those who guided me, as slender as was my hope, my most acute problem was my personal reaction. I did manage to live with my shameful fear to be known as a cardiac case, but I suffered to some extent almost every day in my life from August, 1931, until February, 1968.

A vast amount of this mental anxiety was unnecessary, even harmful. The best thing I did was at the same time the worst. I kept my anxiety almost entirely to myself. Apart from an occasional crying out for help—as I had to the men with whom I stood in line seeking that LOP job—I suffered in silence. This was good, I feel, because it kept me from complaining and criticizing. When I wrongly felt the problem was the fault of other people, I kept my opinion to myself. The good factors in this approach were that I did make a nuisance of myself, and I did not load others down with my problems.

But while I can see one small advantage in being secretive about my rheumatic heart condition, I can now see several disadvantages. For one thing, I discovered that in ignorance and silence fear miltiplies. I often felt worse off than I was. Again, I missed, through almost total silence, help which I could have secured as I grew older. If I had been alert, I could have found doctors, ministers, teachers, and friends who could have given me information and comfort. Both of these would have made my mental load lighter. For most of the time from age twenty to age thirty-five, I was too tied up with my problem to risk it in dialogue with anyone able to help me. Those were fearful and shaky days!

NOTES

[1] The book *Today's Health Guide*, published by the American Medical Association, edited by W. W. Bauer, M.D., has furnished much data to aid me in accurately describing my various heart problems.

Chapter IV
WALKING IN SHADOWS

In 1931 I had rheumatic fever, and in 1943 I entered the Christian ministry. During those twelve years I acquired a number of bad mental and emotional habits. The painful circumstances which caused me to acquire these bad habits at times all but defeated me. Moreover, these habits posed serious barriers to my new-found desire in 1943 to break out of my self-imposed bonds and to be of service to God and man.

Some wonderful grouping of God's grace, the encouragement of family and friends, and some personal pride and stubornness combined to lead me to a new way of life in 1943. I have been forever grateful to God, family, friends, unaccounted-for circumstances, and some deep inner resources of strength—all of which led me to take one of those leaps of faith which mark clearly the boundaries between eras in the life of a person.

But now let me ask you to walk with me through some dark shadows during my teen years.

Smothering Protection

When school started in September, 1931, I missed the first several weeks—six to eight, as I recall. In a small town—Bossier City had three to four thousand people then—if one person was ill, all the folks in town knew it. It was no surprise that all of my classmates in the fifth grade knew that I had been ill. *They knew that I had had rheumatic fever but not that I had heart damage.* They also knew the exact day I was to return to school.

I can recall the scene vividly. I walked the three blocks from my home to the school grounds, picking up two classmates on the way. When we arrived at the gate to the fenced area of the school, seven or eight others were waiting. For a few minutes they gathered about me, patting me on the back and all trying to ask questions at the same time.

Only one specific remark remains with me to this day. One boy said, "We're glad to have you back, and we're not afraid of you!"

I have no memory of what I said to him, but I have deep impressions of shock. Why, I wondered, should he be afraid? Of course, at that time I had no idea how contagious streptococcus infections were. I also had only the slightest understanding about the relationship of this infection to my rheumatic fever and heart problem. So I really did not understand why he should fear me.

I often brooded about that remark. Had my teachers told the kids that I was not now dangerous, but that I had been? Had their parents warned them to leave me alone? I did not know, and I was afraid and ashamed to ask.

Gradually I was dropping a cloak of secrecy about my illness. I had served my sentence of bed rest with only a fair attitude. When you were ten, it was extremely difficult to spend 90 percent of your time in bed during August, September, and October. And much of the company I had were adults, with a few older teenagers who were friends of my sister. Kids of my age were not encouraged to visit me.

By the time I returned to school that fall, I was a changed person. My health was forever changed—for the worse. My attitude was only fair at best. I had started the habit of hiding information about myself when I could. I had started learning how to avoid questions about my health, how to twist answers, and even how to lie with a straight face if no other answer was readily available.

To hide information, to twist answers, and to lie when necessary saved me pain, frustration, and embarrassment. These statements are written with a sense of shame but also with a feeling of release that I can see now what I was doing then. I was wrong, but I couldn't do otherwise then—I thought.

The people who could have helped me—my parents, doctors, teachers, church leaders, older adults—were, I think, as misled as I. They all seemed to be engaged in a conspiracy "to protect" me from additional harm. They simply did not know how to help a rheumatic fever patient. Clear-cut understanding of ways to help people like me was decades away. I write these words not to condemn but to explain. Not one of these persons ever deliberately did one thing to hurt or hinder me. Not one!

I did have a real medical problem, and I did get the best help available at the time. I'm convinced now, after living with heart problems for forty years, that my own negative, secretive reaction to my problem was worse than the physical problem itself.

In the years from 1931 through June, 1938, when I graduated from high school, I remember many times being embarrassed by teachers, friends, doctors, and parents. These unpleasant experiences usually took the form of some type of smothering overprotection. I was occasionally pulled out of schoolground games by a few overzealous teachers. I was often discussed in the presence of others as some adults would explain to one or more that I had a "bad heart" and could not do certain things.

These experiences caused me to burn with anger. I secretly wished that people would mind their own business. I'm sure now that that is exactly what they were trying to do, but I did not like it.

Tough Competition

In day-by-day living I could not compete equally in physical activities with my friends and classmates. In prolonged physical exertion, in extremely rough physical games, and in organized high school sports I was deficient. (I am speaking of the years I was thirteen to sixteen years old.)

My deficiency in sporting activities caused me sharp pain. I deeply loved sports—any and all of them. (And I still do!) At the top of my ambitions then was the intense desire to be an athlete. *But my rheumatic heart problem prevented me from any serious effort at being one.*

As all the guys did, I played various games. I did so against doctor's orders and my family's wishes, but I played. We played "sandlot" football games on vacant lots; "pickup" softball and baseball games on dirt streets or empty lots. We improvised track meets in alleys or wherever space was available. We played "shinny" (roller skate hockey) with crooked tree limbs on quiet residential streets. We played tennis on Wilhelmina Street (where my home was located) and other concrete streets. We played volleyball and a new "coach-created" game of "volley-tennis" on the schoolgrounds.

My love for sports and those sandlot activities caused me to be misunderstood many times. I should not have played football and similar sports because they were dangerous for one with a heart problem. We used no equipment whatever in sandlot football. Skinned elbows and knees, sprained ankels, bad bruises, broken teeth, black eyes, and other assorted minor injuries were common. I don't recall that any of our crowd ever got seriously hurt, although tragic accidents often happen in sandlot football. I know now that I could have done many things then, but football should not have been one of them. Yet I loved to play.

Among the sandlot crowd I was the best punter, kick-off man, and extra-point man. By personal choice I usually played left end. Decades before Coach Earl (Red) Blaik of Army invented the famous split-end, I played a form of "split end" in order to stay out of the heavy traffic of the line play. Sometimes I would even catch a pass! Warnings from family and doctor did not stop me, but they did make me cautious. This caution sometimes brought ridicule upon me.

When I finished high school, I was six feet tall and weighed 130 pounds. These statistics are important in relation to the most embarrassing moment I think I ever had. In regard to playing football, I would have been at best a candidate for the third, fourth, or fifth team even if I had had no heart involvement. Bossier City had some good football teams, and a person with my limited physical endowment had no chance to play football. Yet, I would have given anything to be able to do so.

One afternoon during the recess period, our high school football coach stopped to watch four of us play volley-tennis. Volley-tennis, as "Coach" conceived it, was played with a volleyball and with a volleyball net strung low on the ground similar to a tennis net. The two courts were marked off like tennis courts. We served the ball and hit returns with our hands. We turned our hands into volley-tennis paddles by various techniques. I put my right fingers on top of my left fingers and inserted my right thumb over my left thumb, under my left index finger, and then pointed my thumb up into the palm of my left hand. This was the grip which our coach had invented, although others would play with one clenched fist supported by the other cupped hand. We served by throwing the ball up with one hand and striking it with the other. We served across court as in tennis, and we counted by the tennis method of 15, 30, 40, and game. "Love" represented zero points.

My partner was Joe Webb Burrage, about 5'6" or 7" tall and weighing about 130–135 pounds. Our opponents were Ed Teague, 6'3", 200-pound varsity football player, and Bobby Hutto, 5'6" or 7" varsity track star in the fifty- and hundred-yard dashes.

Joe Webb, Ed, and Bobby were among my best friends. Ed and Bobby were the two best volley-tennis players in school. Joe Webb and I met them in the school finals in the spring, and we lost.

Losing to Ed and Bobby never came easy to me, even though I had had lots of experience at it. They had beaten R. C. Hutto (Bobby's big brother) and me for two straight years in the finals, and they beat Joe Webb and me in the spring finals of 1938.

I have never fully understood the incident which happened that afternoon. Watching us play that day, along with our coach, were a few dozen or more of our schoolmates, some of whom were our best and most admired high school athletes.

As our head coach watches us play, I noticed that he kept looking at me. Ed Teague was already one of his brightest football stars. Joe Webb and Bobby were really too small and too light for varsity football. I guess—and that's all I can do because Coach's remark has never made sense to me—that my six feet misled him. I have thought of that scene hundreds of times. I have had in past years some hostility and resentment about it. I now blame myself more than the coach for this incident.

Once, when it was my turn to serve, I took the ball and went to the base line. Just as I paused before throwing the ball up, the coach spoke to me loudly enough to be heard by the twenty-five or thirty people standing around.

He asked, "H. C., how come you don't come out for football?"

I stopped, looked at him, and felt my face turn red in anger and embarrassment. It seems to me as if I stood there a full minute before answering, and all those present seemed to pause to hear what I would say.

Finally, and with difficulty, I replied, "I don't come out for football because I don't like football!" This was, of course, a big lie. I felt that I did not have the talent, size, or health to play football. But I could not say the words. I just couldn't admit openly that I had a "bad heart" and limited athletic talent. Some of the onlookers knew I was lying, but I couldn't bring myself to tell the coach the truth.

Coach snapped back sharply, "Well, H. C., that's one way to hide the fact that you are a coward!"

The words stung. Some of the fellows laughed, and several aloud said, 'No!"

That scene has been frozen in my mind since those September days in 1937. The thought still hurts.

If I could just have faced up to the fact that I had a rheumatic heart, I could have answered the coach honestly, "Coach, I want to play football, but the doctor won't let me!" That simple, honest answer would have left no scar, but I couldn't say it!

I know now that, whatever his reason was for asking me to play football, the coach would have accepted that answer. He was a good coach and a fair one. I'm positive now that he did not know about my heart involvement. I'm also sure that he instinctively knew I was lying. He knew how much I loved sports, and he knew something about my ability to play volley-tennis. He set up the school rankings each spring for volley tennis. For three straight years he ranked Ed Teague first, Bobby Hutto second, and me third. (He also ranked the Teague-Hutto doubles team number one for those years and the Hutto-Brown team number two for two years, and the Brown-Burrage team number two for one year.)

The coach was goading me for some reason, but I never did find out why. Certainly, he knew that I could do his football team no good.

After sharply challenging me, the coach walked off. When he did, Ed Teague ran over to me and asked, "Why didn't you tell him you can't play footaball?" I just shook my head. I was too embarrassed to reply.

Ed's older brother, Arthur Ray Teague, was one of my bosses at Barksdale Drug Store, where I worked afternoons and nights for about three years. Arthur Ray Teague and J. D. "Dutch" Fenton were pharmacists and co-owners of the drug store. This store was the center of social, political, and sports gossip in Bossier City for several decades. By working at Barksdale Drug, I received a wonderful education pointing toward "common sense" during the years of midsummer, 1935, to August, 1938.

Ed Teague, who also worked at times as a delivery boy and soda jerk, had heard from his older brother about my heart condition. On that embarrassing occasion Ed challenged me to tell the coach. I refused. Then Ed said that he would tell him. I strongly argued the point that I didn't want the coach to know. As far as I know, the coach never learned the truth. I found a real sense of irony in the fact that a decade or so later the coach himself developed a serious heart problem.

It was tough to be challenged and not be able to measure up. It was tougher to be falsely called a coward. From this perspective, in the fall of 1971, it is also tough to look back and see how easily I could have answered honestly and simply without misunderstanding. But I had built up a false sense of shame which overpowered me.

As you can understand, I received a lot of flak after that run-in with the coach. One interesting thing about this verbal abuse stands out in my mind. Not one bit of it ever came from any varsity athlete. I'm sure that they knew that a tall, skinny guy like me could do little to help them. The verbal thrusts came from some fellows I ran around with from time to time. None of them was any better endowed physically than I was. They were all athletes of the sandlot like me. I did not have judgment to face that fact then. But from this perspective in 1971, every name which comes back to my mind was about as unqualified for high school athletics as was I.

I have learned one thing from this observation: It makes

a real difference who is criticizing you. If the person is qualified to judge you, you can give more weight to the criticism. If, however, the one doing the criticizing is not qualified, he should be ignored or forgotten. I would have saved considerable inner anguish if I could have observed the simple truths of this paragraph when I was ten to sixteen years old.

Some Minor Accomplishments

I dreamed dreams of being a great athlete, but there was not the remotest chance that I could have been. I did not have the physical endowment, and I did have a fairly serious heart problem. There just was no way I could have been a high school, college, or professional athlete.

I made up for my lack of physical prowess by an open and enthusiastic admiration of many great athletes, talented sports writers, and exciting radio sportscasters.

Sometime between my tenth and sixteenth birthdays, I decided that I would be a sports writer. If I couldn't be an athlete, at least I could write about athletes. Thus I transferred my eagerness to an attainable area. This was the beginning of a wholesome solution to living with heart problems, and I regret that I waited so long to complete the adjustment. Even after I decided to become a sports writer, I still could not and would not remove the cloak of secrecy from my shoulders about having heart problems. Another day, another disease, another disaster, and other decades would pass before I could finally adjust to living with heart problems.

During these troublesome years I found joy in admiring great teams and athletes. This love of sports went on to become a lifetime hobby.

Bobby Hutto and I were not only intense rivals on the

volley-tennis court; we competed constantly to be the best informed on sports statistics. In order to do this, we both memorized such things as the lists of all American and National pennant winners, home run hitters, batting champions, and dozens of other such lists in all major sports.

We would test each other constantly—in hallways at school, before school, after school, and at just any opportunity—by asking each other questions. Bobby asked me one day, "How many home runs did Babe Ruth hit in his third, fifth, seventh, and ninth years in baseball?" He hoped I would ignore Babe Ruth's pitching days in Boston and start with his Yankee years. I didn't forget, and I knew the answers.

One day Bobby and I found a magazine containing a lengthy sports test—one hundred answers were called for. A grade of 50 was passing, 70 was above average, and a grade of 80 or above—said the magazine—qualified one to be a professional sports writer. The questions were difficult. Who were Yale's first three all-American football players? Who were the men who had hit four home runs in one game? Who were the men who pitched more than one major league no-hit game? And there were others.

I made 87. Bobby made 92.

As hard as I studied, he always stayed a little ahead in mastering sports statistics—just as he did on the volley-tennis court.

Much of this sports information has "stuck" in my mind over all these years. Recently, to test myself, I wrote out the American and National baseball pennant winners for the last fifty years. I have always had difficulty in remembering a few pennant winners during the mid-1920's and mid-1930's. I made a grade of 97 on this simple 100-point test.

If I had spent as much time and energy during my high school years studying "quality subjects" as I did learning sports data, I would have enriched my life enormously. But I would have missed a lot of fun then and a lifetime of enjoyment since! Would I change all this if I could relive those days?

I'm not sure—I'm really not sure.

I needed an emotional prop badly in those days, and sports statistics provided this support. I have fought, bled, and died in my struggles to equip myself mentally for the Christian ministry; many of these intellectual battles could have been avoided or easily won if my younger years had been wisely used. In spite of this fact, I doubt now that I would do these particular things any differently. I did seriously need a sense of accomplishment in something, and sports statistics gave me this opportunity.

I have dwelt at length and in complete honesty, I think, about my actual lack of physical ability to be an athlete. Yet, there were *a few minor accomplishments,* of a physical sort, which give me a warm glow even today.

First, along with my friends Ed Teague and Bobby Hutto, I joined the Red Shield Boys' Club of Shreveport, Louisiana. This club, sponsored by the Salvation Army, arranged various types of activities for the boys. One highly successful program was the volley ball contest each spring. Ed, Bobby, and I made up three of the starting members on one team. The spring of 1937, our team won the Red Shield Boys' Volley Ball Championship of Shreveport and Bossier City. I earned the only gold medal of my life—a gold-placed replica of a volley ball.

Second, in one of our neighborhood track meets, I pole-vaulted eight feet with an old cane pole which was about nine feet long. One of our crowd had found a fishing pole which was about three times larger than a regular fishing pole. We taped this pole very tightly and heavily at all the joints with electrical tape. In fact, most of the top three or four feet was covered by tape. This may sound like a strange vaulting pole, but it worked. Most of us in that particular neighborhood track meet weighed from 90 to 130 pounds. I guess I was at 125 to 130 pounds, about as heavy as anyone using the pole. With it I once managed to vault eight feet. Our pit was the hard ground—no pads, mats, air cushions, sawdust, foam rubber, or even sand.

Fortunately for me—or unfortunately—one girl watching that afternoon was a high school yell leader. She couldn't have it any other way, she said, but to tell the coach. She wanted me to go out for the track team.

Eight feet is not much for pole vaulting. Men are high jumping their way toward eight feet now. But I wanted to try. So the girl told the coach.

He stopped me one afternoon and said, "I hear you can vault a little."

"A little," I replied.

"Why don't you come out this afternoon and let me see what you can do?"

With hesitation I said, "OK, I'll try!"

That afternoon I got about a ten-minute trial. I flunked. The regular cane pole in use in those days was too big and heavy for me. I felt like a mouse trying to run with a baseball bat.

I couldn't get over eight feet with that big pole—nor even seven feet.

This ended my try-out for varsity sports.

However, as dismal as was that showing, I had actually

vaulted eight feet with a "home-improved fishing pole"!

It doesn't take much to make some folks happy!

Back I went to sandlot track meets. At least I was the best at some things there!

Third, I have already related the fact that I was for three years the third-best volley-tennis player at Bossier High School. And my partner and I (one partner for two years and another for one year) were the second-best doubles team for three years. This game was lots of fun and provided me with some inner sense of accomplishment.

Fourth, I have saved for last the tastiest moment of pride in a small physical accomplishment. We grew up on skates in Bossier City during the 1930's. I had learned to skate on our front porch when I was about six or seven years old. We had skate races, skate relays, skate hockey (we called it "shinny"), skate car-hopping, skate firecracker wars, and other skate games.

Skate car-hopping, we thought, was lots of fun. We would skate around cars stopped for the traffic light at the foot of the bridge connecting Bossier City and Shreveport. The traffic light on the Bossier side of the bridge was only about fifty feet from the bridge. As the cars stopped for the light and then started up somewhat slowly, we would grab the rear end bumpers (they did have bumpers then!) and the cars would haul us up the bridge. This gave us a ride to the top at ten, fifteen, or twenty miles-per-hour. We counted this great fun, as well as saving ourselves the trouble of having to skate up hill to climb the bridge. Not one of us ever got hurt car-hopping. It was dangerous, but I guess we were too young or too stupid to know it.

Getting the free ride to the top was fun, but it was a prelude to the point of getting there. After several of the gang had hooked rides to the top of the bridge, we would usually spend some time in a bull session and some time watching the Red River at night. I always thought the river looked beautiful with its swirling dark red colors and the waves reflecting the lights and moonbeams. The Red River, flowing south down from Texas-Oklahoma-Arkansas, separated Bossier City and Shreveport. The red clay and sand in the water gave the river its name.

After all the gang had reached the top, we would proceed one at a time to take a run down the bridge sidewalks. Few people walked the bridge sidewalks at night, so we almost always had them to ourselves.

This skate "rocket ride," we called it, always reminded me of the downhill ski runs we would see occasionally in the Pathé newsreels at our local (ten cents admission) theater. I do not know just how fast we travelled, but a guess is that we often reached speeds of fifteen to twenty—or more—miles per hour. I judge this by the fact that we held our own with cars coming down the bridge into Bossier City. There was no speed limit on us except the natural laws of wind resistance, gravitational pull, and frictional resistance between skates and concrete.

The automobile speed limit on Bossier City's side of the bridge was 23½ miles per hour! I do not know what the speed limit is now, but for decades it was 23½ miles per hour. I thought that was amusing even when I was fifteen years old. Still do, in fact!

We would take our bridge run on skates at what was for us a very high rate of speed. The object was to be able to make the fairly short rounded curve in the sidewalk at the bottom. Immediately after the curve the sidewalk ended in a mound of dirt which had apparently been left there following construction of the bridge during 1932-1933. This mound of dirt was two to two and one-half feet high.

When we negotiated the curve—if we made it up-right—we had to jump the mound of dirt and run on our skates in the dirt side street which intersected the bridge at the traffic light.

Sounds silly, doesn't it? Well, it was. Yet, I recall only one injury of any consequence during several years of these downhill skate runs. One fellow lost two teeth one night when he tripped going into the curve and plunged into the concrete wall bordering the sidewalk. Of course, we had lots of skinned knees, elbows, ankles, and occasionally a skinned nose and forehead when we would fall on our knees and roll forward to "plow the concrete" with our noses and heads.

One reason we had no serious injuries was that only the best skaters in town tried the down-the-bridge run. A second reason was that all the fellows I recall skating with were careful and discriminating skaters. There is a big difference between taking some small chances and being stupid and reckless.

All of these details are background for that one warmest moment I ever had in physical activities. It came in a game of roller skate hockey or shinny. In our roller skate shinny we made no effort to play by rigid hockey rules. We made up our rules. No one ever wrote them down. We just remembered and taught each other from season to season. I guess they were a modified form of ice hockey rules. Since I skated the year round, and especially in the fall, winter, and early spring, I think I had my best athletic ability on skates. For our puck we used a tin can which we beat into a metal ball. I developed some talent for skating and keeping the metal ball under the control of my shinny stick. I also acquired some skill in skating backward in order to defend against an attacking player.

During the Christmas holidays of 1937, we played a lot of shinny on Wyche Street, which had little automobile traffic. On this particular day I wish to tell you about, about eighteen to twenty guys wanted to play. Several varsity football, boxing, basketball, and track athletes from Bossier High were in the gang that day. Among them were an all-state football player, a star running back, a star track man, and a state high school middle-weight boxing champion.

After a group discussion we decided to choose sides by allowing Richard (Ric) Bond and another varsity athlete to pick the teams. Richard and the other guy, whose name I have forgotten, tossed a shinny stick to see who would get first pick. Richard Bond tossed his stick to his opponent, who caught the stick in the right hand. Ric put his hand on the stick over the other guy's hand, and the opponent then put his hand over Bond's. They walked their hands up the stick this way fist by fist until only one could get a grip on the stick. Ric Bond won the toss.

He looked over the crowd and *picked me first.*

Man! Man, oh man!

That was one of the most exciting moments of my life.

You need to have a few facts about Richard Bond in order to understand my delight. Ric, one of four or five Bond brothers who were star athletes at Bossier High School over twelve to fifteen years, was a hard-hitting running back. He was not big by standards of the 1970's—about 5'10" and 160 pounds—but I think that he was one of the toughest and gutsiest high school athletes I ever knew. He was the kind who, as coaches liked to say, "loved to hit people!" and he did hit them. He would hit the line and run head on into 250-pound giants because the play called for it. He would do this again and again in a game.

Richard Bond was one of those athletes I would have loved to be able to imitate. But I couldn't.

Yet, Richard chose me.

One critic in the crowd who was a "sandlot athlete" like me—and my constant rival in almost everything—said to Richard, "You can't pick him. There are eight or ten guys better than he is."

Ric had been born with a split lip—called "hare-lip" in popular terms—and we often had trouble understanding him.

He shook his head and said as distinctly as he could, "I've been watching you all play, and H. C. is the best player on the street!"

Man, I felt eight feet tall! I would have tried to run over a 250-pounder myself for a team captain like that.

I am pleased to report that Richard's team easily won the game.

This delightful incident followed by three or four months my run-in with the coach. I felt that Richard Bond, by his confidence in me, helped me vindicate myself.

By every normal sensible and medical standard, I tried to do many physical things which were beyond my ability and which were actually dangerous to me. Yet, I couldn't seem to help it. I bitterly resented having a bad heart, and I had a terrible attitude of secrecy about it.

These "illicit" sports activities, I think, constituted most of my youthful rebellions. I did much to injure my health, but I also did much which helped to keep me from being a quitter—a cardiac cripple who couldn't face up to life.

Chapter V

WALKING IN THE TEETH OF THE WIND

Several critical crises pressured me considerably during the years 1943–1968. These pressure points made my heart problems more difficult. Moreover, these crises occupied me to such an extent that I often could concentrate only upon the event of the moment. All of these tensions kept me from settling down to fight and whip the lifelong fear I had to be known as a cardiac case. The longer I lived with this emotional hangup, the more deeply entrenched it became.

When pressure is added to many forms of physical illness, the result usually is a deteriorating physical condition. Several times in my case my heart condition became more complicated in the face of another tragedy. As my physical condition deteriorated, my fears about it grew and grew.

Clifton Scott Brown. December 27, 1954—February 24, 1955

Scott was born two days after Christmas, 1954. He made things interesting for us on the 24th, 25th, and 26th.

Young ministers and their wives have a saying about their babies: "These babies are usually born in the early hours of a Sunday morning when the expectant father is out of town in a revival meeting." Well, my two children did not follow that rule. Kay was born about 10:00 P.M. on December 19, 1950; and Scott was born about 9:00 P.M. on December 27, 1954.

Before Kay was born, I had absolutely no preference as to a boy or a girl. My simple prayer was that my wife be all right and the baby be normal and healthy.

Mary Kathryn (Kay) Brown was so born.

Clifton Scott Brown was not so born.

The night Scott was due, A. D. and Mary Langston, Billy Wayne Hollaway, Waynon Mott, and two or three other friends waited with me at Harris Hospital. The birth was expected between 8:00 and 9:00 P.M. As the minutes ticked past nine, I got more and more nervous. I had always heard that there is no more useless person living than an expectant father. I decided that night that the old saying was correct.

Finally, about 10:00 P.M., I looked down the hall and saw Dr. Claunch coming. I quickly stood up and stepped through the swinging doors into the hall to meet him. Something about the way he walked disturbed me. He had his head down and did not look up until I called his name.

This had not been the way it was when Kay was born. On December 19, 1950, Dr. Claunch had come striding briskly down the hall, head erect, and smiling broadly. That walk told me Dorothy Ruth and our new baby were all right. Indeed they were!

But the night of December 27, the scene was different. I said, "Dr. Claunch!"

He quickly looked up, took my arm, and led me down

the hall away from those waiting with me.

He said quietly, "Dr. Brown, Mrs. Brown is all right, but we are having trouble with the baby—a boy."

I felt sick all over.

Dr. Claunch said, "The baby is having serious difficulty in breathing, and his heart is not normal!"

"Oh, my God," I cried in my inner self, "he is a blue baby!"

And he was.

Specialists were consulted, numerous tests were run, but the verdict was that Scott had deformed lungs, heart, feet, and perhaps even brain damage.

Dorothy Ruth and I cried out to God, "How? Why?" Oh, how we prayed for answers and help for Scott!

In the end there was nothing—absolutely nothing—which could be done for Scott.

Through the help of Dr. Claunch, the baby specialist, and others, we did find out what could have caused the tragedy.

When Dorothy Ruth was about five or six weeks pregnant and not yet aware of that fact, one night she went to visit a friend who lived near the campus of Southwestern Seminary.

When Dorothy Ruth walked up on her friend's front porch, a little dog bit her on the right leg. The bite did not appear to be serious, but Dorothy Ruth visited the doctor the next day to be sure. She had been severely bitten by a vicious dog when she was ten years old, and she still had some anxiety about dogs and dog bites. She had the bite checked and treated, and was given a tetanus shot as a matter of precaution. She had no reason to think she could not take a tetanus shot.

That night, several hours after taking the shot, she began to swell about the face, body, hands, and ankles. The swelling stabilized itself shortly; so we went on to bed. By the next morning the swelling was gone. Nevertheless, we checked with the doctor again and found out that she had had some type of reaction to the shot.

We thought nothing more about the tetanus shot or the swelling until after Scott was born as a "blue baby" with critical and inoperable problems.

Dr. H. W. Anderson, our pediatrician, asked us dozens and dozens of questions. His sure and persistent probing finally turned up the experience of the dog, the bite, the tetanus shot, and the swelling.

When we recounted this story, he said, "Well, it looks to me as if we have found the possible causative factor in the birth defects of your baby." He explained in detail that the swelling of Dorothy Ruth's face and body had probably cut off oxygen to the fetus. He could only guess, he said, as to how long the fetus had been deprived of oxygen. It was his judgment that cutting off the oxygen supply to a fetus could and probably would result in some serious type of birth defect.

Dorothy Ruth and I accepted this explanation at face value. We were considerably startled, therefore, one day during Scott's stay in the hospital—he spent every day of his two short months in the hospital—when a friend challenged the doctor's opinion.

This friend said, "Don't let that doctor fool you. He doesn't know why you produced a baby with serious birth defects. He was just looking for something which sounded reasonable, to try to calm your anxiety."

I found this attitude difficult to understand. I did believe the doctor. I saw no reason not to. I have had doctors I didn't particularly like, some who angered me much, and a few I felt would soften their words rather than frankly facing a difficult truth with me. But I have never had one—and I have had dozens in the years between my tenth birthday and today—who I thought told me a lie. Not one! I say this with some anger, because rather than the doctor's being unfair to us, I felt that that friend was unkind and not a little cruel.

The day I checked Dorothy Ruth out of the hospital stands out vividly. I paid our bill, went after the car, and picked up Dorothy Ruth at the exit where she was waiting with the nurse's aide who had brought her down. We got in the car and drove toward our home at 4145 Sixth Avenue. We were going south on Fifth Avenue; and as we crossed Elizabeth Boulevard, we both just broke down and cried. I pulled over to the curb until I could compose myself. We were going home without Scott. And we both knew that he would never go home to 4145 Sixth Avenue.

Scott died on February 24, 1955. We took him back to Bossier City for burial on February 27.

After we returned to Fort Worth following the funeral, we picked up the pieces and tried to carry on as best we could. We seemed to move in a vacuum most of the time.

On Sunday morning, several weeks before Easter, 1955, Dorothy Ruth, Kay, and I got up, had breakfast, and dressed for church. As we walked out the front door, I noticed that the sun was shining beautifully. I had not seen it for months.

I looked at our front yard and noticed something I had not seen since the previous September. I turned to Dorothy Ruth and said, "Look! The grass is green again!"

How beautiful the world looked! I was deeply moved by the thought that in the midst of all of our sorrow and sadness God does live. God's world had gone on living; and it was alive, bright, and beautiful. The sunshine warmed the cool spring morning, and the grass was a fresh, bright green.

Subacute Bacterial Endocarditis. April–September, 1955

The two months Scott was in the hospital, our family tried to carry on their work to the best of their ability. During this time I became extremely fatigued. Excessive fatigue is a deadly enemy of a cardiac case. I should have pulled back after those two exhausting months, but I did not.

Somehow, I felt that I would live a better Christian life and please God more if I would carry on my full work of teaching at Southwestern Seminary. I also continued to preach at various churches when I was invited to fill the pulpit. I recall going to south Texas once; to Houston, Texas, twice; holding a revival meeting in a church in the southeastern part of Fort Worth; and preaching in Grapevine, Texas, twice.

The second time I visited the church at Grapevine, the Sunday before Easter, I recall feeling somewhat feverish and nauseated. I did not think too much about it that morning, but I became very aware of having some kind of respiratory infection as I tried to preach. My face felt flushed and hot, and I had difficulty in speaking. By the time I got home for lunch—about 12:45 P.M.—I felt nauseated. After lunch I rested until 3:00 P.M.; but when I awoke, I was worse.

I called Dr. Claunch, and he asked me to meet him at his office. He took my temperature, and it was 102 degrees. He checked my throat and said, "You've got a bad strep throat!"

A person who has had rheumatic fever with resultant

valve damage is about as safe playing with rattlesnakes as he is with a strep throat. Dr. Claunch began a program of penicillin treatment immediately, but I was already seriously ill. After several days of home and office treatment, I was taken to Harris Hospital.

A full-course treatment was given to me to defeat the strep throat. After about one week, the laboratory tests showed that I was able to go home. But twenty-four hours after going home, I began to run a low-grade fever. For a month I worked with Dr. Claunch and Dr. Fershtand, but my body would not respond to treatment. Again I was taken to Harris Hospital.

This time an extensive series of tests were run. It became apparent that I did not have a renewed attack of rheumatic fever, but subacute bacterial endocarditis. This serious cardiac disease, prior to the discovery of sulfa drugs, was almost 100 percent fatal. Dr. Fershtand later told me that there is a large volume of medical literature on various treatments which have not proved effective on subacute bacterial endocarditis. Sulfa drugs brought a small amount of relief. Penicillin proved to be the medicine which could and often did work.

At the time of my second hospital visit, I had never heard of subacute bacterial endocarditis. Gradually, I learned a few basic details about this illness. Subacute bacterial endocarditis, as I understood it, sometimes followed a previous rheumatic fever incident. This disease, triggered by a streptococcus or staphylococcus infection, attacked old rheumatic fever scar tissues in the heart. Like bees making a bee hive, the strep or staph germs gathered in clusters upon the heart valves and proceeded to destroy them. Dr. Fershtand one day drew a simple sketch of the way my heart valves would look under a powerful microscope; the drawing resembled clusters of grapes. The "grapes" in this case were millions of strep bacteria feasting on my heart. In a nonmedical figure of speech, those bacteria literally "ate up" my heart valves before the doctors could drive them out. Even though doctors had learned to whip this disease with penicillin and a battery of other so-called miracle drugs, it often did additional damage to one's heart.

My second visit to the hospital lasted six weeks. During this time I took countless shots, swallowed hundreds of pills, and endured dozens of blood tests. I tried to be a cooperative patient but I think that I only succeeded in a small way. I began to get angry at the slow progress I was making. I stupidly started trying to second-guess Dr. Claunch and Dr. Fershtand and even tried to tell them what to do. I stayed in a constant argument with my wife, my mother when she came to visit, my friends, and some of my students who would complain about grades. (These students didn't know how ill I was.) I was in no condition then to help others with their problems; mine were sitting too heavy on me! Fears and anxiety were eating me up, but I wouldn't allow myself to talk about them. I still would talk with only a few people about the fact that I was waging a serious cardiac battle for survival. Of course, I talked with Dr. Claunch and Dr. Fershtand, the nurses, and my wife. I could also talk with a close friend, Dr. Gordon Clinard, a fellow minister who taught homiletics with me at Southwestern Seminary.

A simple, honest facing of my cardiac problems would have helped me immensely. I have never asked Dr. Claunch or Dr. Fershtand, but I am now convinced that my inner turmoil about my serious illness contributed to my slow progress toward recovery.

On July 1, 1955, I was released from the hospital. All the laboratory tests showed that subacute bacterial endocarditis had been knocked out. However, within forty-eight hours my fever returned, and I developed a serious type of erratic heart rhythm.

Back to the hospital I went, for the third time in a matter of three months. This time I was to stay for about three months before I could go home cured.

A miracle of medical care, God's grace, and factors unknown allowed me to get well. At the time I had subacute bacterial endocarditis, a young soldier at a nearby Air Force base was also treated for this dangerous disease. Dr. Fershtand treated both of us and used approximately the same treatment on both. The soldier was several years younger than I, was in much better general health, and had the advantage of the same doctor and same medical treatment. By all standards of medical judgment I should have died and he should have lived. Yet, he died and I lived. Such happenings are beyond the discernment of our finite intelligence. We can only weep about one and rejoice about the other.

This long bout with subacute bacterial endocarditis did extensive additional damage to my heart. It also further damaged my self-confidence and my willingness to trust my problems to other people.

Dorothy Ruth (Ware) Brown. 1924–1966

After my first wife died on November 7, 1966, a young colleague of mine at Southwestern Seminary said, "Looking at you and Dorothy Ruth these last two or three years has been to me like watching someone drown and not being able to help. It was agonizing!"

From 1962 through November 7, 1966, Dorothy Ruth

suffered one type of illness after another. Nephritis—a serious kidney disease—finally took her life.

In 1967 I wrote the book, *A Search for Strength*, to share the battles our family fought before Dorothy Ruth's death and those Kay and I fought after her untimely passing. I suggest to you that if your burdens or fear center around illness and death, you read *A Search for Strength*.

This next statement is not a complaint but a simple statement of fact. During the years Dorothy Ruth was ill so much of the time (critically ill during 1965–1966), I became utterly exhausted. If she had not been so desperately ill and needed so much constant care, I would have been forced to get treatment myself for heart exhaustion. Kay was between her eleventh and fifteenth birthdays. I felt that there was just no way I could add the burden of an ill father who had to be hospitalized to the burden she already was carrying of having a seriously ill mother.

I deliberately chose to carry on. Finally, my heart did fail me, fifteen months after Dorothy Ruth died.

Again, this is not a complaint—I would not do it any other way again; yet my two serious illnesses (1955 and 1968) followed periods of fatal illness for my son and my wife. I simply did not have the physical stamina or heart power to keep going without becoming ill myself. And my extreme secrecy about my heart problems added intense pressure to my already overloaded heart.

During the 1962–1966 period, our family was like a runaway train going downhill without brakes to stop it. I felt that we were like an airplane diving toward the ground without power to pull out. I could see only tragedy in a matter of time, but I felt powerless to act.

A Big Lonely House. November 7, 1966—November 18, 1967

When Dorothy Ruth died at 5:55 P.M. on November 7, 1966, at Harris Hospital, Dr. Claunch was at her side. I stood on the other side of the bed. In *A Search for Strength* I wrote these words:

> On November 7, 1966, at 5:55 P.M. in Harris Hospital Fort Worth, Texas, Dorothy Ruth Brown went home to be with God. In the two years she was seriously ill, she made adequate preparation for any eventuality. For one thing, she asked me not to leave her as long as she needed me. I told her that I would always be with her. At 5:55 P.M. on November 7, 1966, she no longer needed me.

And I wrote these words:

> One Saturday night near the end of her physical life, she thought she was dying. At 8:00 P.M., when the time for the five-minute visit came, she talked to me about death. When the five minutes passed, just as the nurses gently motioned us out of that room of critically ill and dying people, she said, "If I don't see you again in the morning, remember that I love you and I have always loved you." She was preparing herself and me for those final moments which were to come all too soon. A thousand times since then, I have been saved from the pit of despair by those words.

And again I wrote:

> When I discussed the approaching end with C. W. Brister, he said, "I do not like the terminology which says that 'God takes people' or that 'God calls people home.' I prefer to say that 'God receives His own!' " I was to find within a few days that this thought would fortify, sustain, and strengthen me in a desperately trying hour.

....

On the night of November 7, shortly before 5:55 P.M., as I gently brushed her hair—one of those little acts which

she appreciated so much—I whispered to her, "I love you
and I have always loved you." I borrowed her words from
a few days before because in those last days we had discussed her use of that precise terminology. The thought
meant much to me and to her. In her last conscious moments, not ten minutes before the end of her life, she
replied with a slight smile on her face, "I love you!"

At 5:55 P.M., as Dr. Claunch stood on one side of the bed
and I stood on the other, she went home to be with God.
I silently whispered my version of the words of C. W. Bris-
ter, "Lord, receive her to thyself in grace, mercy, and
peace." And it was so. There was deep sorrow in my heart,
but it was mingled with God's amazing grace. There was
peace in that room! In those moments, she looked more
beautiful to me than in all the past twenty-one years of our
married life.

Hours, days, and weeks blended together following
November 7, as family and friends did all that love could
do for Kay and me.[1]

Family and friends can do much for a family who have
lost a loved one in death. They can do much and ought
to—for a long, long time. But still there are many things
which the family must do for themselves. There is no way
that anyone can, or should even try to, take the place of
a deceased child, husband, wife, mother, or father. The
family must make peace with the fact that the loved one
is dead.

Peace and acceptance must come. This takes time. No
one knows how much time is needed, but time must pass
before healing can occur in the face of death. Friends and
family can help, but the basic healing will come within the
individual as he faces the issue, turns to God for grace, and
trusts him for strength.

It is easier to write these words than it was to live them.
It always is easier to talk about making peace than to do

it. But the person who faces the death of a loved one must make peace with death, or he will destroy himself, his family, his work, and his creativity.

I had to make peace with Dorothy Ruth's death. I determined to carry on my work as a teacher at Southwestern Seminary to the best of my ability, to continue to teach the Business Men's Bible Class at Broadway Baptist Church each Sunday, to write and edit as I had time and strength, and above all to be the kind of father to Kay I should be.

The days following November 7, 1966, were long, blue, and lonesome. By personal choice I came home at the end of each day's work and attempted to read, do research, and write. These things helped, of course, but there were times I felt so lonesome I thought I would choke.

Kay was fifteen years old when her mother died. As you know, youth has a lot of recuperative power. Her friends, I felt, were unusually kind and thoughtful to her. She received numerous offers to go to all kinds of girl get-togethers: slumber parties, cookie-baking parties, Christmas parties, music parties. And she dated, also.

There were times, when she had an invitation to go out, that I wanted to cry, "Please, Kay, stay here! I need you; I need you to talk to me; to be with me, to just be here in this house!"

I never once said those words!

I knew I had my adjustment to make, and she had hers. I felt that to have kept her at home would have helped me temporarily, but I wondered what it would have done for her. So I let her go with her dates and her girl friends. And I am glad.

I believe that she developed and matured between her thirteenth and eighteenth years. These years, among others, included the two years her mother was critically ill, the year we were alone, and the year following. And I feel she has continued to develop beautifully.

There were lonely nights, however, when I felt that this house would swell and swell until it appeared to be as big as a football stadium and as empty as a football field is at 3:00 A.M. You can be so lonely and grief-stricken that you can literally feel the despair of that loneliness.

Heart Exhaustion. 1962–1968

The constant strain of Dorothy Ruth's problems drained all the physical reserve I had. Moreover, the year Kay and I were alone added to the depletion of my strength. On November 18, 1967, I married Velma Lynn Darbo, whose coming into our home brought an end to loneliness and some relief from exhaustion. However, I was so far "over the hill" physically that I could not stop the process of heart failure from occurring.

At the beginning of the spring term in January, 1968, at Southwestern Seminary, I was so near physical collapse that I could barely manage to get to my classes. In each class I followed the same routine. I took my coat off and sat down to teach. Shortly after the beginning of the term, one young man—whose name I have never learned—wrote me the following unsigned and undated note:

DR. BROWN:
It is quite disappointing and really disgusting to see a professor at Southwestern Seminary teaching in his shirt sleeves. I was expecting it to be quite different. Is there no place for dignity anymore? I think there should be—and one of these places is in our classrooms here. The rooms where you and the others teach are year-round air-condi-

tioned, and there is no excuse for your lack of manners and dignity.

A Student

This was the first anonymous letter I had ever received. Even though it was rather mild in comparison to the usual anonymous letters people get, I reacted with considerable hostility. My first impulse was to check all papers which had come to me—some assignments had to be typed—to see if I could match the typing. I quickly decided that such a procedure would be silly. My next impulse was to read the note to the class and ask the writer to come visit me without fear of reprisal, a reprimand, or a "professorial lecture." But this procedure would involve having to tell the student about my health problem; so I decided to do nothing. I would just wait and see if anything else developed.

Something did develop, but it was not what I had in mind. I had heart failure shortly after I got the note and never appeared before that class again. Of course, the note had nothing to do with my heart collapse.

My mind convicts me again at this juncture about just how easily such a bad situation could have been avoided. I could have told the class in January that I had a difficult heart problem which caused my heart to run in my body like a hot motor in a car. As a consequence, I became tired and drenched with perspiration upon the slightest physical, mental, or emotional activity. Talking, dialoguing, debating, and preaching are strenuous activities. It is my conviction—and so I teach my students—that the average speaker will expend as much energy in making a thirty- to forty-minute speech as a workman will use in eight hours of physical work. But since I was so reluctant to be known as a cardiac case, I could not make such a simple, honest declaration to those students.

All during this period (1962–1968) my energy level rose and fell like a person on a seesaw. It fluctuated from near exhaustion to medium energy, depending on the amount of sleep and rest I could squeeze in. But a rested condition —in the sense of being able to relax and face with assurance one's tasks—always seemed to be just beyond where I lived and worked.

My heart failure really was a normal result of my health problems and manner of living. I see now how heart failure might have been avoided, but at that time I could not clearly see such a fearful and dangerous result until I was at the point of death.

In this chapter I have tried to share several acute crises which tended to help destroy my already damaged heart and which drove even deeper underground my fears to be known as a cardiac case. Following heart failure on February 8 and April 28, I began to break out of my bonds of fear and anxiety. In those two experiences when I was so very close to death, I was literally given a "new heart" about my heart fears.

NOTES

[1] H. C. Brown, Jr., *A Search for Strength* (Waco, Texas: Word Books, 1967), pp. 10–13.

Chapter VI

WALKING TOWARD THE SUN

One road leading to Glacier National Park is called "the Going to the Sun Highway." This picturesque name is as beautiful as the setting. The route crosses some of the most magnificent scenery in America on its way across the mountains. Since I first traveled "the Going to the Sun Highway," I have thought of that beautiful journey as a picture of victorous living. Keep that picture in mind as I share with you a number of victorious periods in my life.

The Miracle of February 8, 1968

As I have related to you, I awoke with acute heart failure on a cold February morning. I was close to death for about twenty-four hours before I began to pull out of the crisis. The skills of Dr. Fershtand, Dr. Claunch, and the nurses and technicians in the cardiac care unit at Harris Hospital all focused on saving my life.

On that morning I somehow summoned faith to tell Dr. Claunch that I was going to live, and that I was committing myself to God and to him and Dr. Fershtand.

Late that night—about 10:30—Dr. Claunch called my

wife to tell her that I was critically ill, but that if I survived the night, there was a good chance I would live.

The first miracle that day was that when I came face to face with death, I also came face to face with the crippling fear I had had for thirty-seven years. I face this emotional demon and slew it! It no longer mattered what anyone knew, said, or did. I no longer cared who knew I had been a rheumatic fever victim for most of my life. When I faced this fear head-on and realized that it could no longer tyrannize me, I won a great victory. In winning this victory, I also helped save my life. Those hours were one of the key periods in my life.

This miracle was the miracle of reality. "Reality" stands for maturity without despair. It stands for maturity with faith, courage, determination, and steadfastness. When I was in Louisiana College in the 1940's, our president, Dr. Edgar Godbold, used to tell us to have "bull-dogged-hang-on-tive-ness!" He said that anyone could quit and drop out, but that it took a person with strength of character to have "bull-dogged-hang-on-tive-ness!" Reality in the face of a serious problem is the ability to have "bull-dogged-hang-on-tive-ness!"

The Miracle of Velma Lynn Darbo

I have related to you earlier that my first wife, Dorothy Ruth, died on November 7, 1966. She spent the last six weeks of her life in the intensive care unit at Harris Hospital. While Dorothy Ruth was there, I could see her only five minutes each two hours. I would spend part of my time between visits working on teaching plans, grading papers, reading for my classes, and writing on an assignment for our Baptist Sunday School Board in Nashville, Tennessee.

The writing assignment was to prepare thirteen Sunday School lesson applications for Bible studies based on the book of Hebrews. These lesson assignments were part of the Life and Work series of Sunday School lessons for Southern Baptists for 1967–1968. The editor of *The Life and Work Annual* for the Baptist Sunday School Board was Miss Velma Lynn Darbo of Nashville.

I had met her by telephone in the fall of 1966 while my wife was critically ill in the hospital. A friend of mine had been given the assignment to write those lesson applications; but because of the press of his work, he asked me to take them over. I accepted the assignment in late August, with a November 1 deadline facing me. About three or four weeks after I accepted these lessons, Dorothy Ruth became critically ill.

I have always tried to carry out my assignments and work as scheduled. But the pressure of having Dorothy Ruth in the intensive care unit from late September until her death almost destroyed my ability to think, to read, to teach, and to write. Nevertheless, I tried to write some material each day while sitting in the halls of Harris Hospital.

I failed to make the November 1 schedule, but I did complete the writing assignment and turned it in to the editor on November 20, 1966. Miss Darbo, through her kindness, patience, and understanding during my days of sorrow, was most helpful to me as I struggled to finish that writing assignment. I undertook it on an emergency basis and had to complete it under what were for me tragic and painful circumstances.

My book, *A Search for Strength*—which was written as a tribute to Dorothy Ruth and as an aid to people with tragedy in their lives—was started on Friday, November

11, 1966. That was the day after Kay and I buried Dorothy Ruth in the Brown family burial plot in Shreveport, Louisiana. I worked along on *A Search for Strength* for months and months. During these months I accepted another writing assignment from Miss Darbo for the 1968–1969 *Life and Work Annual.*

Over the months a friendship developed with Miss Darbo which, as time passed, grew and grew. I asked her to edit and check my book, *A Search for Strength,* because I came to have a high respect for her editorial and rhetorical skills. Eventually, I made several trips to Nashville concerning writing assignments and publishing matters, and I began to see Miss Darbo socially. We fell in love and were married on November 18, 1967.

Her coming into my home filled a huge vacuum. My daughter Kay had known Velma Lynn Darbo for years before I did. Kay knew Velma through her editorship of the youth magazine, *Upward,* a Baptist Sunday School Board publication, and through her column of advice to teen-agers. Among many Southern Baptist teen-agers Velma was known as "Lynn" because of this column, which was called "Letters to Lynn." She was sometimes called the "Baptist Ann Landers."

Kay was the first to know that I had become interested in Velma Darbo. I took Kay to the Colonial Cafeteria one night after I was sure that I was going to date again. While we ate dinner, I told Kay about my plans.

I said, "There will be people who will not like the fact that I am going to begin dating Miss Darbo, and I wanted you to know about this matter first. How do you feel about this?"

She replied, "Daddy, I will fight for your right to date and even to get married. You have a right to a life of your own, and I will stand with you."

Kay was sixteen.

I was so very proud of her love, confidence, and concern. And I rejoiced greatly in her maturity in the face of the difficult times we had been through.

I said to Velma one day, shortly before we were married in San Angelo, Texas, by my long-time friend, Gordon Clinard, "You know, I think that the sermon by Harry Emerson Fosdick on *Handling Life's Second Best* describes both of us. Dr. Fosdick in this message (one of the greatest sermons in print in the English language) preached about the apostle Paul and his desire to take the gospel to Asia. God hindered him and sent him instead to Macedonia, to Europe. Fosdick said that Paul made the best out of a second choice. He took this second choice and made of it a beautiful thing."

I said to Velma, "You and I are trying to do this. It would have been best if you could have married when you were in your twenties and have lived happily with your husband and children, if any, all of your life. You did not marry until your mid-forties, and you are now trying to make a beautiful thing out of a second choice. As for me, it would have been best for me and for Kay if Dorothy Ruth could have lived out her full life instead of dying at forty-two. So, I too am trying to make a beautiful thing out of a second choice."

Velma agreed. This may sound strange, but this is the way life is. A friend told me that I should not have used this illustration with Velma because it didn't sound right to refer to our marriage as a second choice. This observation, however, is not true to the facts of our lives nor is it true to the way life is. We often—and I do mean *often* —have to live our lives on the basis of a second, a third, a fourth, or even a fifth choice. Making the best of our available choices is part of this honest reality I came to understand after Dorothy Ruth's death, my two heart failures, and heart surgery.

Velma's coming to my home was providential in its timing. Less than three months after our marriage, I suffered acute heart failure. When I realized that morning that I couldn't breathe and that something was happening to my heart and lungs, I awakened Velma.

I said, "Velma, wake up! Wake up! Please call Dr. Claunch! I can't breathe!"

As I recall the scene, she didn't say one word. She sat up in bed, reached over to the phone on a bedside stand, and dialed Dr. Claunch. She told him what I had said.

He apparently asked her what position I was in—I had stretched out across the bed—because she turned to me and said, "Dr. Claunch said for you to sit up!"

Velma and Dr. Claunch talked for a few minutes, and he assured her that he was on his way to our home to help.

I have often thought of Velma's conduct on that fearful morning. I was grateful then, and I am even more so now, that she didn't "go-to-pieces," start crying, or ask questions. She did the thing I asked in the shortest possible time.

I am also pleased to report that Kay conducted herself with calmness and maturity. She had lost her mother fifteen months before; now she faced the imminent loss of her father. At all times Kay and Velma were towers of strength to me. They acted with faith, calmness, and love. Their conduct during those crisis-filled months was as helpful to me as the skilled medical attention I received.

One of the warmest memories I have of that fearful February day is a conversation between Velma and Kay the first night I was in the hospital. Dr. Claunch had called Velma about 10:30 P.M. to tell her just how sick I was. She sat down with Kay to tell her the whole story.

I had never told Kay about my heart problems under the mistaken impression that I could protect her from needless anxiety. I should have shared the basic facts with her. Again, my morbid fears prevented me. So Velma had the task of explaining my history of heart trouble as well as informing Kay about my critical condition.

Kay's first impulse caused her to say, "It's not fair! It's just not fair." She was naturally concerned about losing her father only fifteen months after losing her mother.

As she and Velma talked, Kay gradually shifted her concern from herself to Velma. She said to Velma, "It must be tough to face losing him, when you've only been married three months." Velma was deeply touched.

Later, when Velma told me about that conversation, I wept in joy for such a daughter.

The Miracle of Life

In frank terms, I should have already been dead five or six times. Well, I know you can't die but once, but there have been at least six times when I missed good opportunities to depart this life. That is, if I had wanted to depart! I have not been anxious to depart! I am not now anxious to leave; and I don't plan to be for another twenty or twenty-five years. As a friend of mine used to say, "I am ready to die any time my time comes, but I am in no hurry! Heaven is my ultimate home, but I am not homesick!" I am in absolute agreement with those two sentences.

Dr. Fershtand told me after I recovered from subacute bacterial endocarditis in 1955, and again after I was beginning to recover from two heart failures and heart surgery in the summer of 1968, "You are not dead because God has not been ready for you to die! He still has something for you to do!"

I said to Dr. Fershtand, "Even though we are members of two different communities of faith [Dr. Fershtand is a Catholic, and I am a Baptist], I surely do like your theological conviction!"

The fact that I am alive to be able to write this book is a miracle.

The Miracle of May 21–23, 1968

May 21–23 were the three most difficult days of my life. You already have the basic facts about my heart surgery on May 21, 1968. There are a few things which should be related about the next three days, which I spent in the surgical recovery room. I feel that it was a miracle that I survived this experience. From this perspective I believe that I could more easily face heart surgery again than I could face another three days in postoperative recovery.

One gentleman in his sixties came by the third or fourth day after I was back in a private room. He, too, had had heart surgery. In fact, he said that this was his second heart operation. His private name for the recovery room was "the snake pit"! He had nothing good to say about that part of his two experiences; but he had generous praise for the doctors, the nurses, and the hospital.

I was taken to the recovery room sometime in the mid-afternoon of May 21. I have a hazy memory about most of the three days in recovery, but I think I awoke around 3:30 P.M. I remember squinting at the clock a long time and finally deciding that it was about 3:30 P.M. I recall thinking, "Well, I didn't die in surgery!"

I also remember seeing and talking with Velma and

with Gordon Clinard for a few minutes about 7:00. Gordon, along with Farrar Patterson, who was later to become a colleague at Southwestern, had come to Houston to sit with Velma during those tension-filled hours.

We had left Kay in Fort Worth with Jana Edwards, the daughter of Billie and Malcolm Edwards; Malcolm is the music director for Broadway Baptist Church. I felt that Kay would be better off in school than sitting in a hospital waiting room in Houston. Besides, I fully expected to come home again—and with better health prospects than when I went to Houston.

The next memory I have of the recovery room was of awakening long enough to discover I was still hooked up to some type of tube and oxygen affair. I had, I think, tubes in my nasal passages and in my throat. When I tried to take them out, I discovered that my hands were tied to the sides of the bed. I tried to talk but couldn't. Finally I started wiggling my right hand at the nurses and doctors who seemed to be all over the place. At last one of the young doctors, seeing me, came to the bed.

I tried to tell him that I wanted the tubes taken out. I'm sure that I didn't make sense, but I'm also sure that he knew what I wanted.

He said, "These tubes are to help you breathe. If I take them out, you will have to breathe for yourself. Can you do that?"

I nodded.

He took the tubes out, and I did continue to breathe. Actually, I had no idea whether or not I could breathe. I have thought since that it is an excellent thing that those doctors and nurses are experts because they don't get much help from the patients—at least, they didn't from me. This was not by choice, but I don't recall having too much capacity for helping.

I asked the young doctor what time it was, and he said, "10:30."

"Morning or night?" I asked.

"Night," he said.

"What day is it?" I asked.

"Tuesday," he replied. "You were operated on this afternoon."

Part of my difficulty with the recovery room lay in the nature of the place and its procedures. The lights burned brightly night and day. The room always seemed to be overcrowded with nurses, doctors, equipment, beds, and desperately ill people.

I must keep repeating phrases such as "I think" and "it seemed to me" because I have been told that most patients seldom understand clearly what is happening. In fact, I have been told that many patients in recovery have hallucinations and other experiences which show a loss of touch with reality. This would not be at all surprising. Heart surgery, in spite of its record of fabulous success, is still a difficult experience. Also, you are a very sick person, or you would not be there. As one doctor said, "An operation is an insult to the human body!" When you add to these factors the nature of recovery rooms, the nature of postoperative recovery difficulties for the human body in any major operation, and the fact that each one in recovery is heavily sedated, you can understand the problems many patients have in the recovery room.

Chaplain Laurence Wilmot, an Anglican minister from England doing research at St. Luke's Hospital, told me later that people who are very sensitive to the needs of others often have special difficulty in the recovery room. This seemed to be true of me, as a minister-teacher. I seemed to be acutely aware of each crying child, of the welfare of the doctors and nurses, and of my own well-being.

In the early morning hours of May 22, I think that Dr. Cooley came into the recovery room. I later learned that he and his team had performed their fourth heart transplant sometime that night. I recall that he checked several patients including me. Then he and several doctors paused near the foot of my bed to talk.

As they talked, something happened to a little girl in the bed next to mine. She had been crying, I think, for hours. At least, every time I knew anything, she seemed to be crying with pain and fright. I knew how she felt. I recall thinking, "Why doesn't someone do something for that poor little girl?" This is not a criticism of the doctors, nurses, or staff. I was hardly qualified to criticize anyone, and I remind you of my previous statements about how difficult it was for patients to be coherent about their recovery room experiences.

The little girl had cardiac arrest, I think. Whatever did happen, it set up a flurry of activity around her bed. I recall that someone worked over her from near my bed, and he bumped my bed several times. I raised up to watch and tried to ask what was happening. A nurse quietly but firmly told me to lie down. She put a hand on my shoulder and pushed me back on the pillow. I tried to get up again and again was pushed down. I felt frantic because I thought that little girl was dying. Finally the doctors straightened up, and I think I heard one say, "She is all right now!" These were terrifying moments for me. They increased my own anxiety.

Cooley and the other doctors again stopped to talk near the foot of my bed. This time I thought for some reason that they were talking about me. I heard one man say, "The valve is ruptured. It will have to come out!"

I thought, "My God, I'm going to have to go back to surgery!" I was terrified. I tried to listen. Then I tried to get the attention of the doctors. I couldn't get anyone to listen to me. A nurse kept telling me everything was all right, to lie back and go to sleep. I remember trying to pray and finally going to sleep.

Later, I awoke to find people working on *me!* I heard a nurse say, "His fever is 106 degrees!" I was burning up. I think, I repeat, I *think* Dr. Cooley was there. They wrapped me in some kind of ice blanket. I recall feeling as if I had just come into a cool room out of a blazing Texas midday sun.

At 6:00 A.M.—visiting hours were 6:00 to 6:15 A.M. —Velma came in. I tried to tell her about my fever. My fever was down, as I recall, to 102 degrees by then, and things were looking up. The doctors did not seem to know why I had this fever.

I also tried to tell Velma about that little girl. She later said I was quite confused about several things, and she was not sure just what I was talking about. We have agreed that the account given above is the way I told it to her then.

At mid-morning, two young doctors came by to check me. One of them told me, "Your heart was a mess!"

I asked him, "Did you help operate on me?"

"Yes," he replied. "I had my hands in your chest yesterday!"

I recall having a squeamish feeling about his descriptive terminology.

One of the doctors in the recovery room instructed me to cough up the phlegm so that I could keep my lungs clear. Several times, nurses repeated the orders to cough. I tried to cough; but each time I did, I felt as if my chest would split open. A sizzling streak of pain, as if caused by a red-hot running (branding) iron, ran from my throat to the lower part of my stomach. After a few feeble efforts at coughing, each time with sharp pain, I quit trying.

A young doctor came to my bed several times during the day and asked me about my coughing. I finally told him that it hurt too much to try.

He looked at me with apparent disgust, turned away, picked up a pillow from a table, and came back to my bed.

He handed me the pillow and said, "Hold this against your chest when you cough, and it will lessen the pain!"

I repeated, "It hurts too much!"

In apparent anger he pointed a finger at me and said, "You are going to lie there and take pneumonia because your lungs are going to fill with fluid. You are going to lie there and die. I have tried for hours to get you to cough!" He walked away. I took that pillow and started coughing! I'm glad to report that his bedside manner, while rough, was just right for me.

Two unique things stand out in my mind about Wednesday night, May 22. I'm reasonably sure from what Velma has told me, what Dr. Painter told me on Thursday morning, and from what I have tried to logically unravel that I must have had some loss of touch with reality.

First, I thought the parents of a small boy kept coming in and out of the recovery room all night, and that they were planning to give the boy a birthday party there in the recovery room. The noise, lights, and laughter angered me, and I registered several complaints. Velma said that at 6:00 A.M. on Thursday I told a somewhat confused story of the happenings of the night.

When Dr. Painter came Thurday about 10:00 A.M. to take the drainage tubes out of my lower abdomen, he asked me about my "nightmare" about a birthday party. I replied with heat that I had heard and seen a birthday party.

He said, "We don't hold birthday parties or any kind of parties in the recovery room. We don't do that any more than you would stage a dance at a worship service."

I still didn't surrender my views of what I thought had happened. I said, "Well, have it your way, Dr. Painter, but they did have a party here last night!"

He shrugged and left.

I also *thought* that a young white nurse kept verbally attacking a young Negro nurse from Africa. It seemed to me that the white nurse criticized her all night long. Two older white nurses got in the act on the side of the Negro girl, and a young intern criticized the young white nurse for her manifest unfairness. I even thought that Dr. Cooley himself came to the recovery room at 2:00 A.M. and questioned the white nurse about the incident.

It is more than likely that since I was so heavily sedated, so tight and anxious, and so racked by pain, I did have something like hallucinations or nightmares that night. I can't prove it either way, but Velma and Dr. Painter both thought that I was somewhat irrational.

A close friend who has had heart surgery since I did says that he also had some hallucinatory difficulties. His doctors told him that these experiences were rather common, and that the primary variation was in the degree of confusion. I thought that I did have those two experiences with a birthday party and a racial argument. I must, however, have been confused that Wednesday night.

I also had several arguments with nurses. The first one

could have been prevented, I think, if I had given adequate information to Dr. Keats, the anesthetist. I got hit in the nose with a baseball when I was a kid, and one of my nasal passages has always been smaller than the other. I remembered to tell Dr. Keats this, but I did not remember to tell him that I used antihistamines for nasal blockage and excessive sinus drainage. When he blocked my nasal passages with tubes and breathed for me with his machines, I did all right. But when the tubes were taken out, my nasal passages blocked and I breathed through my mouth. When this happened, my mouth dried out.

Thirst is a problem in the immediate postoperative period and it became annoyingly so to me. I asked repeatedly for water. The nurses said no. As I understand their answer now with a four-year perspective, the reason was that water would have made me extremely nauseated so soon after surgery. Apparently I did not fully understand this, and I continued to ask for water. One nurse said in exasperation, "Stop complaining so much and go back to sleep!"

After I had several verbal rounds with different nurses about water, Dr. Cooley told one nurse to give me a towel with crushed ice in it. He allowed me to suck on the ice and thus relieve my thirst.

The second general disagreement I had with the nurses in the recovery room came on Thursday morning, May 23. Velma had told me that morning at 6:00 that I would be placed in a private room one day early because of the hard night I had just had. I was not given any details because they had not been worked out. In a state of confusion about when I would be moved, I asked the nurses a number of times when I would go to my private room. Apparently I angered two of the nurses by asking so many questions. They both, I thought, lost their tempers and criticized me for bothering them when they had so much to do.

I recall feeling both anger and shame about these two encounters with the nurses in surgical recovery. I was angry because I did not understand exactly what was going on, and I was embarrassed because I apparently angered several of the nurses by asking too many questions. Chaplain Floyd later told me that such experiences were fairly normal due to the natural state of tension which existed in that critical situation. He was generous in his praise for those hard-working women in surgical recovery who did their work in a "life and death" situation. He brought light and understanding to me in what had been an extremely difficult and highly confused state of affairs.

Again, I feel fortunate to have lived through the postoperative period. I reacted rather negatively to that experience. Considering the seriousness of my heart problem, the risks following double-valve surgery, the fever crisis with 106 degrees, and my continual emotional disturbances with the nurses and doctors in surgical recovery, I count it a miracle that I survived those three days.

The Miracle of Postoperative Recovery

Postoperative recovery took multiple forms during the forty-two months following heart surgery. Recovery for me has never been a straight line upward or downward. It seemed to be an up-and-down path which led gradually upward. But the path did lead upward.

Over the first forty-two months following surgery, I was hit with anemia for about one year, a number of urinary infections, bursitis in my left shoulder in the spring of 1971, bursitis and adhesive encapsulitis in my right shoulder for about one year in 1971, numerous back muscle spasms, two abcessed teeth with resultant root canal work, and numerous sinus and respiratory infections.

The most serious postoperative problems I had were three incidents of cardiac fibrillation: the first period of irregularity of heart rhythm following surgery, from October 1968 until April, 1969; the second brief period of fibrillation occurred in November, 1969; and the third period of fibrillation occurred in Agusut, 1970. It lasted one week.

First, in October, 1968, I developed a heartbeat irregularity. Dr. Fershtand treated me with rest and special medication, and I made considerable progress toward reacquiring a normal rhythm. But because the irregularity continued, Dr. Fershtand asked me in April, 1969, to return to Houston for what I thought was my first experience with electric cardioversion. This is an electrical shock treatment which is designed to restore the natural rhythm to the heart.

My wife and I drove to Houston on a rainy Saturday and checked into the Tidelands Motel, managed by Dickey Maegle, the former Rice University and San Francisco professional football player. This motel serves the hospitals of the Texas Medical Center. Velma and I wandered around St. Luke's Hospital on Sunday afternoon, renewed our friendship with Dr. Louis Leatherman, one of my cardiologists; Mrs. Reed, head nurse on the third floor where I had a private room following surgery; and several other staff people.

On Monday morning I reported to Dr. Robert Leachman; I was delighted to see him. Patients who have been near death and have had good doctors who helped restore them to good health develop a warm appreciation for those doctors. Dr. Leachman examined me carefully, asked a series of questions, and checked the data sent to him by Dr. Fershtand. He said that he would use cardioversion to restore a normal rhythm to my heart. He put me on a hospital cart and told me to take off my shoes, shirt, and glasses. I was anesthetized and given the needed treatment.

I felt the shock. I recall gradually going to sleep. Then suddenly I saw a bright silver flash which engulfed me, and I "imagined" I saw the hind legs of a mule kicking me in the chest. I had the feeling that my chest was crushed. I recall saying—or thought I said—"Uh!"

When I awoke I was lying *peacefully* and *relaxed* on the cart in the room where the cardioversion was done. I looked a few feet to my right and saw Dr. Leatherman sitting with his back to me at a typewriter.

When he heard me stir, he turned around and grinned at me. He said, "Do you know what I think?"

"No!" I replied softly. I felt as relaxed as one string of well-cooked spaghetti.

He said, "I think that we just shocked the devil out of the Reverend Mr. Brown. What do you think?"

"Doctor, I hope you did," I replied. "Because if you really did shock the devil out of me, you will save me lots of struggles with sin!"

"Glad to be of service," he replied with a chuckle at our corny humor.

Later, several of my colleagues on the faculty of Southwestern Seminary told me that they would like to buy one of those machines. When I asked why, one said, "Just think of what kind of evangelist I could become if I had a machine which could shock the devil out of people! Why, I could become as famous as Billy Graham!"

The doctors checked me out and released me.

I went back to the motel as if nothing had happened —and promptly came unglued. I felt again as limber and loose as that well-cooked spaghetti. Velma and I had planned to go home the next morning; but because I felt so totally "unhinged," it was Thursday before we could return to Fort Worth.

I told you a few paragraphs ago that in April, 1969—the one just described—I had my *first* experience with electric heart shock. After having this experience, I recalled something that had happened in surgery. I had had a similar experience with being engulfed with a bright silver flash. At the time of surgery it made no particular impression on me because so many other things were also happening. The April, 1969, cardioversion dragged out of my subconscious mind the events of May 21, 1968, when I also saw a silver flash and felt as if someone had hit me across the chest with a baseball bat.

From April until November, 1969, my path of medical progress seemed to go steadily upward. Suddenly, one Sunday morning, as if someone had thrown a switch, I felt a "nerve flash" go all over my body, and my heart popped out of rhythm. I was hospitalized the next day for tests. On Tuesday morning, Dr. Fershtand said, "I think you can have the cardioversion here this time. You are one and one-half years from surgery, we know much more about your condition, and we have several expert cardiologists in Fort Worth who can do cardioversions."

He named about five or six cardiologists he could recommend. One name he called was Dr. Bobby Brown. I asked, "Is this the same Bobby Brown who was the Yankee baseball star?"

"Yes," he said.

"I would like to have Dr. Bobby Brown," I replied.

I had heard good reports about his medical skills, so I trusted him. The fact that he also was, for me, a "glamorous, talented ex-athlete" compelled me to ask for him.

That Tuesday afternoon Dr. Bobby Brown came into my room at the Boulevard Hospital. He entered the room and said, "I am Dr. Brown."

I replied, "You are the 'Golden Boy of the Yankees!' "

He said with a slight grin, "I am just a tarnished image of his former golden glory!"

He, Velma, and I laughed.

I had the feeling again that I had at St. Luke's: "Well, if I couldn't be an athlete, I can be friends with several great ones!"

He sat down calmly and said, "Tell me about yourself."

I wanted to talk baseball. So we spent thirty minutes talking about Casey Stengel, Yogi Berra, Whitey Ford, Mickey Mantle, and other great Yankee players.

Finally he began asking me questions about my heart problems. I think he gave as sharp an oral examination as I have ever had. Then he checked me carefully. He said, "I think I am going to let you go home for a couple of days and then ask you to report on Thursday morning to St. Joseph's Hospital for the cardioversion."

I made one request of him. I said, "If you can do so safely, I would like to be anesthetized enough so that I will not feel that electrical shock."

He said that he would see what he could do, but that such results were not always possible.

He added, "We'll both just do the best we can; and if we do that, I'm sure it will be satisfactory."

On Thursday morning I checked into St. Joseph's for the cardioversion. By the time I was prepared by the nurses, Dr. Brown came.

He used three different shocks of, as I recall, 100, 200, and 300 watts-seconds.

I am happy to report that I did not feel any of them. When I awoke I was totally relaxed and as loose as a rubber band which had been overstretched until all the tension was gone.

From November, 1969, I went until August, 1970, with cardiac regularity. But that August my heart popped out of rhythm for the third time. For some reason, this experience got to me. I had been more or less calm and matter-of-fact about the first two incidents of cardioversion. Again, as in the first and second incidents of cardiac fibrillation, my heart got out of rhythm on a Sunday. On Monday I checked with Dr. Fershtand. He tested me and said, "Come back tomorrow for further tests."

I did. The electrocardiogram confirmed that my heart was out of rhythm. So, back to bed I went until Thursday, at which time I again checked into St. Joseph's for cardioversion by Dr. Bobby Brown.

By 11:30 A.M. that Thursday, I was prepared by the nurses for the doctor. But because of several medical crises, Dr. Brown was about forty-five minutes late in getting to St. Joseph's.

By 12:45 P.M. I had grown quite tense. I was extremely annoyed about this third cardiac irregularity. Coupled with my inner frustration was the long wait at the hospital. I had told the nurses, when I checked in, that Dr. Brown would be along any minute. In order to save his time— during his lunch period—the nurses had hooked me up to the cardioversion machine. The longer I waited, the tighter I got. The tighter I got, the more I dreaded the possibility of feeling those shocks. I had had five previous shocks of which I had felt the first two. The memory was distinctly unpleasant.

Finally Dr. Brown came. He apologized for the unavoidable delay. When he put me to sleep, he had to use about twice as much medication as he had the previous November because of my "wrought up" condition. Again he gave me three shocks. Being in such an uptight condition, I felt the second and third shocks. And they hurt! Again, with both shocks I felt as if my chest had caved in.

Now the record was four periods of electrical shock (counting surgery) with a total of eight individual charges. Of these eight I have felt four. That's batting 500! However, in this game the way to win is to get your heart back in rhythm without feeling the charges. At least that would be the way I would like to play the game.

It has now been fifteen months since I have had cardiac irregularity. The doctors interpret this as a good sign. However, no one can know just when or how often a person with my medical history will go into cardiac fibrillation. I hope the answer is "very seldom!"

My recovery from two heart failures and open heart surgery has been miraculous. It has not been easy! The path has been up and down and up again. I am grateful that the path has been mostly up. I plan to keep it that way.

The Miracle of Communication

I not only broke the bonds of the fear to be known as a partial cardiac cripple; I developed a desire to share the good news.

Dr. J. P. Allen, my pastor at the time of my first heart failure, told me that he visited me three times while I was in the cardiac care unit and that I told him each time about whipping this fear. The interesting thing about this is that

I do not remember seeing or talking with J. P. Allen even one time while I was in the cardiac care unit.

My entire personality—conscious and subconscious— burst out in a rush of thanksgiving for the joyful victory. For me to be able to tell this good news to everyone was truly miraculous! Whereas, previously, I could tell only a trusted few people, I now wanted the world to know that I had a new and glorious victory in my life. I wanted to "shout it from the housetop!"

One fact reveals to me that I had broken the back of my "sick secrecy" about my heart condition. Between February 8 and June 2, I wrote letters telling the "whole truth" to President Robert E. Naylor of Southewestern Seminary; to each faculty and staff member at Southwestern; to each student in each of my classes; and to the members of the Business Men's Bible class at Broadway Baptist Church.

I would like to share with you parts of some of these letters. I believe they will show you clearly my change of attitude toward my heart problems.

The first is taken from a letter written on March 11, 1968, to my faculty colleagues:

> Guess what happened to me while teaching one semester in a "little old easy seminary position"! As we have always heard, "anyone can teach in a seminary, but it takes real 'intestinal fortitude' to work and serve in the churches."
>
> *One,* years ago when I was somewhat younger than I am now, I had rheumatic fever, which left me with a scarred aortic valve (the big, funny-looking one coming out of the top of the heart). *Two,* this resulted in a shortage of physical energy for me through the years. This explains why I often sit down to teach, ride the elevator rather than running up the stairs like some of our young "Jack Armstrongs," and never walk anyplace if I can help it. *Three,* because

of items *one* and *two*, I have practiced to some extent
restraint in regard to extra and outside activities at the
Seminary. *Four*, in 1955 I had a prolonged bout with a
"strep" infection which caused additional heart damage.
Five, during the last five or six years crises by the score
have hit the Browns—and these multiple events drained
away almost all my physical reserve. *Six*, in late December,
1967, I had a bout with a virus infection. *Seven*, again on
Thursday, February 1, I started a second bout with a virus.
Eight, thus it was that on February 8, 1968 (Thursday), I
was unable to breathe properly when I awakened at 6:00
A.M.

Dr. Claunch thought for a few hours that I had taken
viral pneumonia, but he soon changed his diagnoisis to
"incipient or early heart failure." Dr. John B. Fershtand,
the heart specialist who was called in for consultation, later
told me that the cluster of things named caused the heart
failure. He said that it was the two bouts with the closely
related virus infections which overpowered me—and, as
he said, "pushed me over the cliff." I was standing on the
edge of the cliff due to items *one* through *five* (listed above).
For about twenty-four hours the doctors did not know
which way I would go; but fortunately the early medical
treatment turned me in the right direction.

Since I have always had fairly serious reservations about
revealing *specific details* concerning my health, and since
several folks have asked for specific details, I now feel that
it could be of some value to share these facts with friends.
Moreover, I trust that with the Lord's help this can be true.
I hope that this letter has not bored you, but rather has
given you some light as to how one of your colleagues could
come close to the brink.

I wrote a similar letter to all the students in my classes.
The basic information given to my students was the same
as that given to my colleagues of the faculty. Prior to these
experiences I would have done nearly anything to hide my
personal problems from my students. The fact that I could

write them about my heart difficulties indicates the extent of my liberation.

Moreover, I added a special section for my students. A portion of that letter follows:

> I commend to you Mr. Gene Hadley [my student assistant]. I know that you will give to him the same generous, kind, and helpful cooperation which you were giving to me. He will give you the best knowledge, guidance, and judgment possible. Gene Hadley has my full and complete confidence, and you will profit much because you have been in his class.
>
> I love my classes and deeply regret that I cannot be present to see you through to a successful conclusion. May I ask that, because of the unusual situation in which we now find ourselves, you make a strong and noble effort at cooperation, listening, participating, and every other aspect of learning. So, when the final chapter of the class has been written, you will in no wise be the loser because of my absence. It would burden me deeply if one man should suffer this term because of my misfortune. Join me in a pledge that this does not happen! Reach out for all the learning that is to be had in this class. I believe that you will do it.
>
> And next year, when I see you in an advanced class or in a graduate seminar, we will be able to move forward together in perfect harmony in our continued search for truth.
>
> Thank you for praying for me, and thank you for all that you are doing to master preaching and to cooperate with your new teacher.

On April 29, after I had had my second heart failure, I wrote a "progress report" to President Naylor. Some pertinent paragraphs show, I think, the distance I had come in liberation from heart fears.

> I had planned today to have my third post-hospital checkup. (Therefore the rough draft of this letter was al-

ready prepared.) You were given a brief report on the first checkup, which was satisfactory, but none on the second because there was nothing new to report. However, rather than having a formal checkup, I had a recurrence of heart failure on Saturday night and am back in the hospital. It is the opinion of Dr. Claunch (my family doctor) and Dr. Fershtand (my heart specialist) that until a few days ago my heart was properly carrying its load under current conditions—mild exercise, regular and sufficient rest, a moderate diet, and routine activities (like watering my trees).

However, both doctors feel that I should undergo a series of tests at Houston within the next week to determine the exact condition of my heart. *This idea is not a new one* but has been in the planning stage since I left the hospital on February 23. These hospital tests will include a catherization of my heart—the most exact form of heart testing known outside of open-heart surgery, as far as I know. The reason for this exhaustive procedure is that persons who have suffered "heart failure" tend to have repeated episodes of heart failure with advancing years. This minor one following the major one within three months indicates the truth of the above statement.

The tests could show, of course, that my heart is stronger than the doctors know and that surgery is not necessary. Nevertheless, I am inclined to accept their joint opinion that the time has come for open-heart surgery. I have thought since 1955 that I would one day have to face this decision. My hope was that it would have been ten or fifteen years hence.

If my doctors are right, and if the tests reveal that I should have this surgery within the near future, I will undergo open-heart surgery at the earliest date acceptable to the doctors. *My physicians here assure me that with successful surgery I will be able to teach in the fall.*

I have worked with reduced heart efficiency for so long that I can get very excited about the prospect of being restored to something like normal health again. I can hardly imagine what it would be like! With nearly normal heart efficiency—or even with a significant improvement—I believe that I could really get some things done. There are many things I wish to do, and I need added strength to do them.

Thank you for allowing me to have this time in order to seek better health. With an improved heart condition I hope to be a stronger teacher and a better servant of Southwestern Seminary and our Lord.

While I was setting my house in order in regard to my family, my seminary responsibilities, and my church work, I wrote one additional letter. This extra letter concerned my hobby of "sports enjoyment." Since I did not *exactly know* whether I would return from Houston alive or dead, I wished to pay tribute to a great man, a great American, and a great athlete. So, I wrote a letter to *Sports Illustrated.* Here is a part of it:

> Respectfully I nominate *Coach Bill Russell* of the Boston Celtics as *Sports Illustrated* Sportsman of the Year for 1968.
>
> Bill Russell is the greatest athlete in America and in the world today. In fact, he has been the greatest athlete in America and the world for the last decade and more. Bill Russell may be the greatest athlete America has ever produced. At the absolute least he ranks with those athletes we call "our immortals"—
> (1) Thorpe, Morrow, Cunningham;
>   (2) Dempsey, Tunney, Louis;
>   (3) Hagan, Jones, Hogan, Palmer, Nicklaus;
>   (4) Cobb, Ruth, Speaker, Feller, DiMaggio;
>   (5) Tilden, Kramer, Gonzales;
>   (6) and on and on.

Now, why should Player-Coach Bill Russell be named *Sports Illustrated* Sportsman of the Year for 1968? I suggest two reasons:

I. Because of personal qualities:
1. Bill Russell is a distinguished American.
2. Bill Russell is an outstanding man worthy of emulation by young Americans.
3. Bill Russell is an eminently fair and just man (while not agreeing with him in all his views of Cassius Clay, I admire his desire to give Clay a fair and just hearing—face to face).
4. Bill Russell is a self-disciplined man dedicated to his work.
5. Bill Russell, as far as I have heard or read and as far as I can see from television observation, is a man free from racial prejudice. A noble virtue in these troubled days!

II. Because of personal performances:
   No athlete in the history of sports has a record to match that of Bill Russell, in both quantity and quality.

In fifteen years involving sixteen major career episodes, Bill Russell has achieved this record with his teams:

First place: 13 times
Second place: 2 times
Unranked: 1 time
             ———
             16 times

This letter is being written as I await a trip to Houston, Texas, for open-heart surgery at the hands of Dr. Denton Cooley on or about May 21 or 22.

Gentlemen, I respectfully nominate Coach Bill Russell of the Boston Celtics to be your Sportsman of the Year for 1968. I confidently look forward to your December, 1968, issue which will announce Player-Coach Bill Russell as your 1968 Sportsman of the Year.

In December, *Sports Illustrated* did name Bill Russell as its Sportsman of the Year for 1968. Therefore, on December 24 I wrote *Sports Illustrated* again.

Letters to the Editor
Sports Illustrated
Time-Life Building
New York, New York 10020

DEAR FRIENDS:

What a Christmas present you have given to the legions of fans of *R U S S E L L   T H E   C E L T I C!*

Your superb selection of Bill Russell as Sportsman of the Year stands and shall stand as a supreme standard for sports selections for several decades!

Bill Russell is the tallest athlete in talent in the twentieth century.

He has never had an equal as an athlete. No sports immortal of the past or present has ever done for his team or for himself what Russell has done.

Congratulations on a superb choice.

Before I went to Houston for heart surgery at the hands of DR. DENTON COOLEY, I set my house, records, work, and affairs in order because even when you face heart surgery with hope, you never know what will happen. One thing I had to do was to express to *Sports Illustrated* my admiration for Bill Russell. (I had never written a real fan letter before, but I felt I had to write one about Russell.) When heart surgery was successful, and after I returned to work in 88 days, I made copies of my letter for seven or eight folks at *Sports Illustrated.* Later I sent about six copies of my little book, *A Search for Strength,* in which I have paid tribute to Bill Russell. Every day which passed caused me to believe more and more that this was to be Bill Russell's year. And this was and is the year of *RUSSELL THE CELTIC.*

Congratulations again on your superb choice of Bill Russell as SPORTSMAN OF THE YEAR.

Cordially,
H. C. BROWN, JR.

One visible sign of a new desire to communicate with others about my freedom from secrecy about heart problems came at Christmas, 1971. I accepted from my family and now proudly wear a sterling silver medical identification bracelet. The bracelet has this information:

Front side

H. C. BROWN	CARDIAC
DR. D. FERSHTAND	817–332–8305
DR. B. BROWN	817–335–6181

Back Side

RH. F. 1931	H. FAILURE '68
H SURGERY '68	QUINIDINE
COUMADIN	DIGITALIS

This bright medical ID flashes from my left wrist—for all to see—that I am a "CARDIAC" who lives by the skill of medical science and the grace of God. This medical ID speaks for me even when I am verbally silent.

This new sign is just one more step in the miracle of communications.

As the story of my problems and victories spread, I began to get calls from people with heart problems. Five or six of these people who contacted me have since had successful heart surgery themselves. I now consider this testimony I have about heart hope to be second only to my testimony of the love and grace of God as we know him in Jesus Christ.

The Miracle of Multiple Victories

All of the words written thus far have discussed one great victory. But there have been more. I have actually won seven great victories over fears and anxieties in the last five years:

1. The fear to be known as a partial cardiac cripple—a 100 percent victory! This has been my personal Exodus!

My day of victory!

2. The fear to be an invalid because of cardiac or other health problems—an 80 to 90 percent victory!

3. The fear to die early, or too early—an 80 to 90 percent victory!

4. The fear of doctors; the fear that they would find something wrong—an 80 to 90 percent victory!

5. The fear to watch, even in movies or on television programs, medical operations or medical procedures—a 99 percent victory.

I haven't yet developed the courage to watch actual open-heart surgery. I told Dr. Leatherman at St. Luke's Hospital that if I knew the particular patient would live, I would like to watch. He suggested that I had better leave the open-heart surgery to the surgeons. I think he is probably right!

6. Anxiety about people over me with positions of authority—a 99 percent victory!

7. The fear to lose a loved one in death—a 99 percent victory.

I have lost by death four grandparents, several relatives, numerous friends and neighbors, many church members, a son, a father, a wife, and a mother. Death never has been easy, and it never will be. *Should I lose by death anyone else dear to me, the pain will be sharp and the loss deeply felt.* Death, however, no longer tyrannizes me! I have looked him in the face again and again, and I know that in Christ Jesus, we who believe in him will win the ultimate victory.

I wrote the above words in October, 1971. At that time I rated several of the seven victories—items 2–3–4—with higher percentages than you just noted. All seven are still great victories for me, but I did lower the percentages somewhat on three items.

The reason for the changes is that recently I have been reading as much as I can about hearts, heart problems, heart surgery, and transplants. As I read some of this material, I found myself tightening up as I investigated the life-and-death struggles of a large number of people who have fought cardiac battles. Some of these people suffered much, and they tragically lost their fights for better health and survival.

For several nights I had some difficulty in sleeping as I went over and over all of the things which happened to these people with sick hearts. I discovered that I was not quite as objective and as removed from the battle as I had estimated in the quiet of my study.

My testimony is still positive, however. It seems to me that one who sets out to share the story of health, hearts, doctors, disease, surgery, and surgeons should attempt to lift a banner which says, "This is the day of hope! This is the way to victory!" I can still say these words with 100 percent confidence.

In my preaching classes at Southwestern Seminary, I tell my young ministers, "It is a tragedy to have nothing to say and to go ahead and say it." I also tell them, "The gospel of Jesus Christ is a positive message which shows forth God's good news for man. The preacher who will not set forth an affirmative message will miss the way. It is the preacher's duty to wave the banner of good tidings from Mount Everest so that all nations, races, and peoples of the earth can see and believe!"

In this book—my good news about hearts—I wish to sound a trumpet and to wave a banner about heart hope. I desire that all who read will respond with faith and hope in our great doctors, compassionate nurses, efficient hospitals, and modern medicine. I have prayed that I would not raise up a foothill when an Everest was needed, that I would not cry wolf when a deliverer was called for, and that I would not speak falsely or maliciously when great affirmations of faith were needed.

As one who has already laid down his life one time in faith that open-heart surgery would provide a better life, I hereby affirm that should the occasion arise when I must have life-saving open-heart surgery again, I would again trust my life to Dr. Denton Cooley and his associates. On the basis of the knowledge I have, I can say the same thing in regard to Dr. Michael DeBakey and other great heart surgeons.

I hope I live to be seventy-five or eighty and that I remain all the while in good health and a useful servant of Jesus Christ. But if not, I have made peace with God, and I trust my doctors!

These, then, have been my "going to the sun" experiences. Even though I have had numbers of hard problems and I have been knocked down for the "eight count" a number of times, there is much to be grateful about. I do praise God for his grace, for skilled and compassionate doctors, for efficient nurses and technicians, for many warm and strong friends, and especially for Velma, Kay, my sister Elizabeth, and all of my other relatives and loved ones.

Remember, there can be a "going to the sun highway" for you.

Come let me travel it with you in the next chapter.

Chapter VII
WALKING WITH YOU

Let me walk hand in hand with you! Let me walk by your side!

No!

No! Those figures of speech are not strong enough.

The warmest thing anyone can say about me is that I relate to them by heartfelt convictions. In 1958, I lectured on preaching at the Mexican Baptist Seminary in Torreon, Mexico. At the end of the week, one young Mexican minister said to me, "I can speak a little English, and I can understand more when another speaks. I want to thank you for sharing your heart with us. You speak with heart power!" I had never heard this term used in just that way. It is a graphic figure of speech.

I am a believer in heart power! I believe in heartfelt friendships, convictions, family relationships, preaching, teaching, working, visiting, and mutual help one for another. With this heartfelt conviction please allow me to help you.

In my struggles with tragedies and fears, I believe I have learned some things about victorious living. Let me help you learn these things. My convictions here will be set out by stating what you can believe and do in order to win victories over your fears and problems.

It helps to believe in God!

I am not talking about "believing" in the sense of just being a member of one religious denomination—Catholic, Protestant, or Jewish. I am talking about the fact that you can lead a stronger, more victorious life if you let God save your soul and direct your life. I am talking about the value of loving and trusting God with your eternal soul and turning over your present life to him. I am not writing to you from the stance of being one member of one particular religious denomination; rather *I am writing to you as a Christian.* My viewpoint is Christian, universal, and eternal. I am interested in your total personality being related properly to the Lord God Jehovah whom we know through Jesus Christ.

How can believing in God help you? As Paul said on one occasion, "Much in every way!" When we believe in God as we know him in Jesus Christ, we have a secured place in eternity. No matter how much some people protest, there is a nearly universal concern about one's place beyond death. I'm reasonably sure that you have thought to some extent about dying and about eternity.

When we believe in God, we follow the Maker and Ruler of the universe. I think most of us have always known that the universe is an immense place, but our picture of it has grown tremendously as each great space adventure of our astronauts has occurred. Almighty God, Creator of heaven and earth, is our ruler.

When we believe in God, we believe in one who is all powerful. Nothing is beyond his ability. Some preachers like to play with sermon titles like "Six Things God Can't Do!" These are trick titles used for cheap publicity and should not be taken seriously. Our God has all power.

When we believe in God, we believe in a God of love. I can recall that this fact moved me deeply as a small child. I have memories which go back to my third and fourth years. My grandmother Yarborough (my mother's mother) used to rock me in a big rocking chair on our front porch. She used to tell me that God loved me. How that made me happy! Then she would tell me about how men crucified, killed, and buried Jesus Christ. She and I would cry and cry. I just couldn't understand how anyone would want to hurt Jesus! Then Grandmother Yarborough would tell me about the resurrection of Jesus and about the love of God for her and me which prompted the greatest message in the Bible. Yes, our God is a God of love!

When we believe in God, we believe in a God of of forgiveness. *God is a specialist in forgiveness!*

One of the strongest contributors to human ills is *the lack of forgiveness* in a person's life. Turn this around and note that one of the healthiest feelings we can experience is the sense of forgiveness.

One thing you ought to do in reading this book is to test your life in relationship to forgiveness.

Forgiveness is triangular or three-dimensional. We need God's forgiveness; we need to forgive others; and we need to forgive ourselves. In order for your total health to be improved by a sense of forgiveness, you need to share in all its aspects.

The basic forgiveness is the one God gives. You know this, do you not? You know from observation, from self-searching, and from deep-down "gut" feelings that you— and I—need God's forgiveness. John wrote it down in his book for us. He said: "If we claim to be sinless, we are self-deceived and strangers to the truth. If we confess our sins, he is just, and may be trusted to forgive our sins and cleanse us from every kind of wrong; but if we say we have committed no sin, we make him out to be a liar, and then his word has no place in us" (1 John 1:8–10, NEB).

Closely related to being forgiven by the Lord, and second only to that forgiveness, is our ability to forgive others and to forgive ourselves. More of us fail in these kinds of forgiveness than in being forgiven by God. As mortals we can cry out to God Almighty and not feel ashamed to ask for his forgiveness. It is infinitely harder, however, to forgive a wife, a husband, a child, a parent, or another relative. It is much more difficult to forgive a foreman, an employee, or a superior. It is much harder to forgive a friend, a neighbor, or a fellow worker.

The people closest to us often wound us deeply. The wounds bleed and they hurt. Because we must of necessity have contact with people—at home, at work, at church, and at play—we will continue to be bruised by them. And of course we do our share of bruising.

At times we find it all but impossible to forgive another person. It is amazing just how much hostility one person can store in his mind toward another. And the feelings of hostility run deep. They remind us of a volcano about to erupt. And erupt these people often do, do they not? These feelings are so fierce and they weigh so heavily on the "carrier" that it is no wonder that they can cause ulcers, intestinal disturbances, high blood pressure, and other tragic illnesses. Hatred can destroy health, family relationships, friends, and careers. To avoid serious results from harboring hostility, we need to forgive others as God has forgiven us. It is not only Christlike to forgive others;

it is infinitely healthier.

To forgive oneself may well be the most difficult of all kinds of forgiveness. It surely has been for me. I do not have the slightest hesitation in seeking God's forgiveness. Indeed, I need his forgiveness daily. But I have considerable difficulty with forgiving myself.

I feel that one reason I was so secretive about my health problems was that I just could not forgive myself for "the way I was." I had to step to the edge of death before I could accept myself as I was. This is reality. It is also self-forgiveness. I had to secure God's forgiveness about the way I was; I had to forgive those who failed me; and above all I had to forgive myself. The dynamic power of triangular forgiveness helped to make me well physically. And it added immeasurably to my inner peace and poise.

How do you rate on forgiveness? Has God forgiven you for your sins, weaknesses, and fears? Have you forgiven those who have hurt you? And have you been able to forgive yourself? Friend, there is peace and poise for you in your struggles with fears when you practice "triangular forgiveness."

No matter what fear, problem, or trial you have, you can defeat it better with God's help. Friend, it helps to believe in God!

It helps to believe in people—family and friends.

What do you think about people? Do you like people? Do you trust people? Do you dare to love people?

Most of us, you see, are usually treated by people according to the way we treat them. You can't make an infallible rule about this. You can only observe that, as a whole, people who respect, trust,—and yes, even love—other people tend to be respected, trusted, and loved. There is something biblical about all this, I think. It must just be one of these universal, timeless truths which God put into his computer when he built this universe and started it out on its magnificent journey.

You can begin by loving your immediate family. This is at once the hardest and the easiest way to love. It is hard sometimes to love our family because the constant friction of minor incidents fray our nerves and make us long to live a separated existence. We do know better, however. We know we were born into a family; we have been matured in a family; we find peace, love, and security in a family; and we will increasingly need a family as we grow older.

Almost as important as family are friends. For people who have lost their families through death, divorce, alienation, or separation of some type—work, geography, or otherwise—friends take the place of blood-ties. One mark of being a mature human being is to desire the friendship of people.

Most of us, however, do not need to choose between family and friends. We can have both. I rather think that God's ideal is that we have both. Family and friends complement each other. This is as it should be. I don't think that I have ever had a physical illness or a problem when I have not been supported and spiritually comforted by both family and friends. For this comfort and strength I constantly thank God.

In working on your fear or trouble or both, learn to respect, trust, and love people—your family and your friends!

What if you have no family? Well, adopt yourself one. I do not mean formal or legal adoption. I mean, just elect yourself a family of people who can walk through this life with you. I have "adopted" in this spirit a couple of sets of grandparents, several sets of parents, a number of big brothers, a lot of little brothers, a few sisters, and cousins by the score to go with my blood cousins by the dozens. And I can tell you truthfully that I have needed all of these people—real family and real friends!

You can do the same thing. You can be a friend and in turn have friends. You can learn to be interested in others. To think about others. To learn to listen to them. To try to think their thoughts. To try to feel their hurts, fears, depressions, and lonesomeness! And as you learn to get friends by being a friend, you will be working to conquer your own fears and problems. It is healing to love and care.

Friend, it helps to believe in people!

It helps to know that you are human.

No one, unless he is mentally sick, really denies that he is human. People do, however, act sometimes as if they were not human. They take no thought for using the fullness of this day, of preparing spiritually for tomorrow, or of facing the fact that tragedy or death could come tomorrow. They are not atheists—they just live as if they were. For all practical purposes they are their "all in all"; they are their own gods!

In a frank face-to-face conversation, this type of person would deny that he holds such views. But he actually does live this way. And the end result is alienation from God, from mature people, and from inner reality.

It helps to know that we are men—human beings—and not God! Not just in words, but with clear-cut, realistic understanding of the fact that we do have limitations. As people with limitations, we are going to fear, get sick, have family fights, suffer doubt and despair, and live with severe handicaps.

It will help us to know that these things—in various ways and degrees—are going to happen to us. And they happen not because God is angry with us or desires to punish us. These evil days will come upon us from time to time because this is one characteristic of being human.

You can probably accept these views now if you do not have a major fear or problem sitting on top of your head. Such acceptance is easy when "all is well." But the mark of success is whipping fears and problems is that you can accept these views as correct when you are "fighting for your life" in a critical situation involving your parents, your wife or husband, your children, your best friends, or your career. You can do so.

Friend, it helps to know that you are human!

It helps to accept your problems as belonging to you.

"Reality" is a great word. The state of living with a sense of reality connotes maturity. Throughout this book I have pleaded for a sense of reality. I think generally that I am a realistic person—sprinkled with a generous portion of idealism. But even though I think that I am a realistic person, I never really faced reality about my heart fear until I had acute heart failure in 1968. I discovered then what "reality" was. I also discovered the joy of victory as I got full release from one thirty-seven-year-old demonic fear.

I do not know what your fear is. I do not know what has caused your burden, broken heart, or battered spirit. I do not know these things in particular, but I do know that you have something "eating" on you! That probably is why you are reading this book.

And I know something else about you. If you can come to grips with your situation as it is, you will take one giant stride toward winning a soul-satisfying victory.

Friend, it helps to accept your problems as belonging to you.

It helps to trust your human resources.

You have resources, strength of mind, and power of character enough to win victories which may have seemed beyond your capacity. You can do far more than you ever dreamed possible if you will turn loose your better self to help yourself.

You have read how my doctors cooperated with God and my body's resources to bring healing to me. Dr. Fershtand and Dr. Claunch, in particular, and other doctors have taught me that they work best when the patient is trustful, relaxed, and cooperating. These doctors insist that apart from the cooperation of mind and body, healing is difficult. On the positive side, healing becomes more likely if all resources of healing are marshalled—the power of God; doctors and medical resources; and the mind, emotions, and body of the patient.

On February 8, 1968, I joined fully in this total team assault on my critical problem of heart failure. I think that this was the first time in my life when I gave unconditional cooperation to God, doctors, medical science, and my body's natural resources!

Success did not have to come. It may not come the next time I have a major medical crisis. It is possible that I—or you—may reach a point of no return as far as immediate physical salvation is concerned. All of us will get to that point of no physical return one day. We all know this.

Yet, the point for which I plead now is that we can drive

fears and problems out of our lives by trusting our best human resources. You can do this if you will just give yourself unconditionally to this attitude of total relaxation, trust, and cooperation.

Friend, it helps to trust your considerable human resources!

It helps to know that qualified help is available to you!

No matter what fear or problem you have, qualified help is available to you. Perhaps I should stress here that I am using "qualified help" in a broad sense. I mean that you can secure help from professional people such as medical doctors, psychiatrists, psychologists, counsellors, sociologists, social workers, ministers, priests, rabbis, teachers, lawyers, industrial chaplains, hospital chaplains, military chaplains, church staff members, nurses and others.

Some of the persons listed above are highly skilled in talking with people with fears and problems. However, some helpers are adequate only for minor problems. These less skilled workers refer serious problems to the more highly skilled people in personality relationships.

Make inquiries about the qualifications of the person whose help you seek. What is his or her reputation? How interested is he in actually helping people? How much time does he have? What kind of professional training has he had? How much and what kind of experience has he had? What fees—if any—does he charge for his service? What is his record of success or failure with real live people with real live problems? Don't feel embarrassed to ask questions. It is your fear, your problem, your personality, and your life. Moreover, it is your family and career and future which are at stake.

One way you can begin is to ask your minister or your

family doctor for help in selecting a highly skilled counsellor. Generally speaking, family doctors and ministers are qualified to counsel, but both groups usually lack the higher technical skills which belong to hospital chaplains, psychologists, psychiatrists, and similarly trained people. Ask your doctor and minister to lead you to a skilled counsellor.

When I was told, in the days following my heart failures in 1968, that I must have immediate heart surgery, my first questions were in what hospital and city and by which doctor and staff. It did not take me long to decide that I wanted Dr. Denton Cooley and staff at St. Luke's Hospital in Houston, Texas. I said to Dr. Fershtand, "Please secure Denton Cooley for me." I pleaded urgently for the best doctor I could get. And, of course, the fact that I am writing this book about heart problems three and one-half years later indicates how pleased I am with my choice.

Let us visit together frankly about securing highly competent professional help. Most folks accept the fact that one can seek out the best medical help available without any type of stigma being attached. It is now commonplace for people all over the world to fly to Houston, Texas, for heart operations at the hands of Dr. Denton Cooley and his associates and staff. This is also true for Dr. Michael Debakey and his associates and staff.

People are applauded for the wisdom, courage, and faith to seek the best medical services possible. However, in the minds of many uninformed people, there is still a stigma about securing adequate help for people with emotional difficulties. A person with a serious emotional problem in his life is just as handicapped as an athlete with a broken leg. A person with a total emotional breakdown is just as ill—or more so—as a man who needs double-valve open-heart surgery.

We must break the grip of gossip, ignorance, and shame about securing adequate help for people with emotional problems and mental illness. You can be one of these people who lets the sunshine of modern medicine, psychology, psychiatry, and counseling shine in your life to bring new physical and emotional health to you, and through you to your family and friends.

Friend, qualified help is available to you!

It helps to dream.

It does indeed help to dream! I do not mean, of course, to "fantasize" or to "daydream" with a complete loss of reality. By "dreaming" I mean to think big, to set goals, to plan, to fervently desire, to plot a path to better accomplishments.

If you dream in this manner, you will be able to visualize yourself with better physical health, mental maturity, and emotional stability. If you dream in this way, you will see yourself as a sharper student of the world around you, as a stronger leader among your peers, as a person of stronger spiritual faith, and as a person of action.

The person who thinks of himself as ill, weak and defeated will act more like an ill, weak, and defeated person. The person who is really ill and has problems can keep from thinking negatively all the time. He can "see" himself overcoming his adverse circumstances. If he holds this higher mental image of himself, he will gradually take advantage of opportunities to help himself.

I grew up with a rheumatic fever heart condition. I was told when I was twenty years old that I would be an invalid at thirty and be dead by the time I was thirty-five. As I have related previously to you, these things seriously handicapped me. They made me fearful and afraid. These stern predictions also deprived me of the ability to seek help which could have released me from my burdens.

At the same time I saw myself as someday succeeding. I always believed that in some way I would have better health; that I would be stronger, that I would learn how to handle my fears and frustrations; that I would be a better balanced, and abler person. I always believed that I would succeed. I always believed that God had something for me to do. My inner mental image was often in conflict with my outer action, and it was often at war with what I really thought of myself. Yet, I never seriously wavered from the conviction that I would whip fears, health problems, tragedies, and trials.

Somehow, someway, I learned "to dream" with a hope. I learned "to dream" with a will to work, to fight, and to persevere. I wanted a better life, and I dreamed that I could have it.

I have had three specific dreams which have stuck with me for most of the last forty years, and they have elevated my life.

My first dream was that I would be a writer. At times I wished to be a sports writer, or a nationally known syndicated writer, or a writer of major articles for big national magazines. These specific dreams have never come to pass. But I have had ample opportunity to write articles for religious magazines and state Baptist papers. Moreover, I have written, co-written, edited, co-edited, and contributed to twenty-five books during the last fifteen years. I think now that the dream of writing that I have had since I was ten years old has been working itself out through these various kinds of writing. I am now in the process of working on five different books at the same time. Without a dream I doubt that I would have ever persevered. I was such a poor writer! No, that is not really an accurate statement! I was a horrible writer! No fooling! I wanted to write—only heaven knows why—but I didn't have a literary background, proper school training, or practical experience! Or anything else to commend me as a writer—except that I dreamed that someday I would be a writer.

Over the last fifteen years I have learned to improve from being horrible to merely terrible, to poor, to bad, to fair, and on up to average. And you know, at times I think (and you must judge here)—at times I think I turn out a sentence or paragraph or even a page of above average material. I actually believe that I have even written a few paragraphs and pages of superior quality material. Now, that's what I think! But please be charitable and remember that I am a dreamer!

In case anyone is interested in testing this out or of checking up on me, please read these books:

A Christian Layman's Guide to Public Speaking

A Quest for Reformation in Preaching

A Search for Strength

Sermon Analysis for Pulpit Power

Steps to the Sermon (with Gordon Clinard and Jesse Northcutt)

Preparing for Effective Bible Teaching (with Velma Darbo Brown)

A second great dream I have had has been to do something to improve race relations among all of our people.

In the spring of 1944, I was a freshman at Louisiana College. Our college administration and student leaders arranged a week of religious activities called a "Focus Week." Among several leaders who attended were Dr.

Clarence Jordon (a pioneer in race relations), Dr. J. P. Allen (then a pastor in Bristol, Tennessee-Virginia), Dr. W. F. Howard (Baptist Student Union director for the Baptist General Convention of Texas), Dr. G. W. Sadler (area secretary for Africa for the Foreign Mission Board of the Southern Baptist Convention), and Dr. Morris Ford (pastor of the First Baptist Church at Longview, Texas).

One sharp area of dialogue centered around race relations. I had never heard Christian leaders, or anyone else for that matter, talk about the total equality of all men under God and before the law. These leaders opened a new world of the oneness of man. I was challenged and thrilled.

One afternoon during that Focus Week, I took my usual afternoon nap. While I was asleep I dreamed a most startling dream! I dreamed that I saw a big black hand and arm come out of some high cumulus clouds, and a big white hand and arm came out of some nearby clouds. I dreamed that God ordered me to reach up and bring the two hands together in a firm handshake of friendship. In the dream I did this—I reached out and took one hand in each of my hands. I brought those black and white hands together in a handshake symbolizing friendship, equality under the law, and equality under God.

The dream awakened me! I sat on the side of my bed for a long time as I thought about that most interesting dream. I quickly recognized that the enormous input I had received that week about the total equality of all people had influenced my dream. I wondered, however, if God had a unique ministry for my life in the area of race relations. Over the years I decided that I did not have a special ministry in race relations, but that I should do everything I could as one person to further the total equality of all men before the law and under God.

I have lived by this code.

I have fought verbal battles with my friends and casual acquaintances over the view that all men are equal. I have been threatened and almost physically assaulted by stating on the streets of a small Louisiana town that Negroes had a right to go to school with whites. I have tried to give a consistent witness to the equality of all men through these last twenty-eight years.

Through twenty-three years I have taught my six thousand students that "of a truth, God is no respecter of persons!" I have urged these young ministers to go forth to lead their churches and communities toward more Christian conduct in race relations. I believe, personally, that "in Christ" we will find better human relationships.

Moreover, I have edited, compiled, and helped to write a book on Christian race relations. This book—*The Cutting Edge*, Volume I—contains twelve chapters on Christian race relations.

I haven't done anything very dramatic in race relations. But as one person with one hammer and one stone chisel, I have cut away at the rock of ignorance and prejudice in race relations. I wish I had done more. *And I will yet do more to serve God and man in the great cause of advancing the true doctrine of the absolute equality of all men before the law and under God.*

My third dream for twenty-eight years has been to be a great teacher. It has been my grand privilege to teach preaching at Southwestern Baptist Theological Seminary for twenty-three years. I have taught about 250 class sections with more than six thousand students. I am still dreaming, working, and praying for wisdom, physical strength, mental discipline, and love of students so that I can indeed be a great teacher.

Some ministers dream of being as talented, famous, and well known as Fulton J. Sheen, Norman Vincent Peale, and Billy Graham. Others dream of being "great preachers," presidents of conventions, and heads of large denominational organizations. Some ministers even dream of making a lot of money. My career dream is to be a great teacher.

Should God grant me the opportunity to teach until I am sixty-five, I will complete thirty-eight years of teaching-preaching at Southwestern Baptist Theological Seminary. I do believe that I have laid the foundation for a creative, loving relationship of teaching. And with God's grace, the cooperation of Seminary leaders and my students, I am going to become a great teacher by 1986!

After all, anyone should learn how to do a job well in thirty-eight years!

It has helped me to dream. I have become a person of more strength, courage, and convictions through having great dreams.

You, too, can lift yourself out of your fears, problems, and burdens by dreaming dreams of victory!

Friend, it helps to dream.

It helps to work!

I am "old fashioned" when it comes to work. For twenty-three years I have taught my students that there are three words which will teach them how to prepare and preach creative sermons.

Those words are:
  Work!
    Work!
      Work!

Work is one way to learn, one way to create, one way to contribute to the service of others, and one way to fight fears and troubles.

Work is one way you can attack your fears and problems. How is this possible?

Work is healing. You can bring calmness to your mind and emotions by engaging in helpful and creative work. As you work you can substitute another person's problems for your own.

I am obviously using "work" in three broad ways: (1) the work by which you earn your living and sustain your family and yourself; (2) the "play-work" you do for fun; and (3) the work you do in service for others. This last is "good Samaritan" kind of work. Which of the three is most important? All of them!

To be a well-rounded, mature person, you must learn to work at a job. If you can learn to enjoy your work, you will be happier and healthier.

You should also learn how to "play-work"!

While I was still in St. Luke's Hospital following heart surgery, Dr. Leachman asked me what I did for fun and recreation.

I replied, "I work. I love to work!"

"Work!" he exclaimed in apparent surprise. "Dr. Brown, work will not get it for you! You must learn to do something for fun in addition to working for fun!"

So, after I returned to Fort Worth on June 1, 1968, Velma and I did a searching analysis looking for "fun things" to take the place of "all work and no play"!

I couldn't run enough, nor did I have enough stamina for running, jogging, or playing tennis. I had never been much at swimming, so that was out. I had previously tried to play golf; but the way I played the game, it was more

of a marathon walking experience while carrying a set of
clubs which I found about as effective as crooked tree
limbs. I once had a 45 for nine holes, and I only broke 50
for nine holes a few times in four or five years. So, golf was
out. It was work-work and not play-work!

One day I got an inspiration. While in my teens I had
loved to play pool and snooker. I had been a fair player;
I could beat most of the crowd I ran around with.

So, pool it was to be. I got my neighbor, Vernon
Meissner, who is a builder and contractor, to convert my
double-car garage into a very nice recreation room. I put
in a ping-pong table (primarily for Kay), a pool table for
all of us and our friends, a dart board, and bookcases. And
I added a king-size bulletin board which I keep half-filled
with pictures and stories about Denton Cooley, his staff,
his hospital, and his patients. I have on the bulletin board
the issue of *Life* magazine featuring Dr. Cooley, Mr.
Thomas (Cooley's first transplant patient), and Mr. Fiero
(Dr. Cooley's fourth transplant patient, who received his
new heart the first night I was in the surgical recovery
room), and two life-size pictures of the mechanical mitral
and aortic valves which Dr. Cooley and associates placed
in my heart.

In addition to playing pool, I also started doing yard
work for fun; feeding and watching birds; collecting rocks;
doing some woodwork; driving in the country to see birds,
trees, and flowers; having more friends in to my home for
pie, pool, and palaver (good conversation and dialogue).
I renewed my interest in magazine collecting and domino
playing; began to study sports statistics again; increased
my participation in TV sports watching; started keeping
card files on stimulating actors and actresses in movies and
television (as part of this, I started sharpening my descrip-

tive writing ability by painting word pictures of people from TV and movies who excited me with their skills); antiquing furniture and chairs (as you do, we have some "ancient modern" things which need dressing up somewhat); and some plain extra resting and sleeping! I can tell you happily that all of these have helped to make my life fuller, healthier, and happier! I am in better health and happier than I have been in twenty-five years. And, friend, I am now fifty years old!

I have continued to try to serve my students to the best of my ability. My students are "my people"! A pastor has a congregation; a medical doctor has his patients; a lawyer has his clients; and I have my students.

My life's priorities are (1) my eternal relationship to God; (2) my relationship to my immediate family (now reduced to three—Velma, Kay, and my sister Elizabeth); and (3) my relationship to Southwestern Baptist Theological Seminary. In regard to the Seminary my priorities are: (1) my classes; (2) my individual students: and (3) my writing ministry.

I am now one assistant Sunday School teacher for the Business Men's Bible Class of Broadway Baptist Church. I taught this class as an assistant teacher from 1963 to 1965, and I was the teacher of the class from 1965 until I had heart failure in 1968. Since the fall of 1968, I have again served these delightful men as an assistant teacher.

Moreover, I have a new ministry of sharing faith, hope, love, courage, and basic "lay information" with people with heart problems. A week does not go by but I have one or more opportunities to tell fearful cardiac patients to trust their souls to God and their hearts to their medical doctors. *I have no medical advice to give.* I try to instil hope and courage in the hearts of the fearful.

You may wish to ask if I have won all my battles with heart fears and problems.

Absolutely not!

But I no longer live a life of fear, shame, secrecy, and morbid dread! This I have decided:

My soul belongs to God. You can't do any better than that!

My physical health—including my heart and its various relationships—belongs to God, to me, and to my talented and dedicated doctors:

Bobby Brown
　DeWitt Claunch
　　Denton Cooley
　　　John Fershtand
　　　　Robert Leachman
　　　　　Louis Leatherman

With doctors like these—they are also my personal friends —you can't do any better than that!

So, when fears attack or health problems arise, I trust the Lord, seek the right help, put on my battle gear, and do battle with renewed faith and courage.

Now, friend, you, too, can work in all of these ways. You can strengthen your attitudes, emotions, and health by doing creative work in all its relationship.

Friend, it helps to work!

It helps to follow the examples of great people.

Friend, do you have a hero?

Or several heroes?

Or even many heroes?

I do. One, several, and many! I have been collecting great people as models, examples, and friends all of my

life. And the harder it took them to become great, the
more I have admired them!

What about you?

My superstar heroes are:

1. *Great statesman*
   Winston Churchill
   Abraham Lincoln
   Thomas Jefferson and George Washington
   Harry Truman
   Richard Nixon

2. *Christian leaders*
   The apostle Paul
   Martin Luther
   John Wesley
   John Jasper
   Billy Graham

3. *Great athletes and great coaches*
   Bill Russell—Red Auerbach
   Vince Lombardi—Bart Starr
   Babe Ruth—Lou Gehrig—Joe DiMaggio—Bobby
      Brown—Casey Stengel
   Ben Hogan—Arnold Palmer—Jack Nicklaus—Gary
      Player—Billy Casper
   Christy Matteson—Walter Johnson—Bob Feller

4. *Creative writers, composers, and journalists*
   Ernie Pyle
   Willie Morris
   Leon Uris
   Harry Emerson Fosdick
   Margaret Mitchell
   Winston Churchill
   Mark Twain
   Walter Winchell

Rogers and Hammerstein
Lerner and Loewe
Johnny Mercer
Irving Berlin
5. *Great scientists*
   George Washington Carver
   Thomas Edison
   Sir Alexander Fleming
   Madame Curie and Louis Pasteur
   Jonas Salk
6. *Show business entertainers*
   Bob Hope—Bing Crosby
   Jimmy Stewart
   Gary Cooper
   Helen Hayes
   Louie Armstrong—Nat "King" Cole
   John Wayne
7. *Military leaders*
   Dwight Eisenhower
   Douglas MacArthur
   George C. Marshall
   George Patton
   Omar Bradley
8. *Civil rights leaders*
   Martin Luther King
   Abraham Lincoln
   Thurgood Marshall
   Roy Wilkins
   Earl Warren—Hugo Black
9. *Explorers*
   Allan Shepard, Gus Grissom, John Glenn, Gordon
      Cooper, Neil Armstrong, and all of our astronauts
   Richard Byrd

Charles Lindbergh
Sir Edmund Hillary and Taning Norkey
Stanley and Livingston

10. *Handicap crushers*
Helen Keller (blindness-deafness)
Glenn Cunningham (critical leg burns)
Ben Hogan (automobile accident)
Jackie Robinson (racial barriers)
Franklin Roosevelt (polio)
John. F. Kennedy (war wounds and religious prejudice)
Bill Russell (racial prejudice)

11. *Zealots who won*
The Adams family of Massachusetts
Patrick Henry
Harriet Beecher Stowe, Henry Ward Beecher, and the Beecher family
Roy Wilkins, Thurgood Marshall, Earl Warren, Hugo Black, and the Supreme Court
Martin Luther King, Jesse Jackson, Ralph Abernathy and friends

12. *Great medical doctors*
Christaan Barnard
Denton Cooley
Michael DeBakey
DeWitt Claunch
Bobby Brown
Robert Leachman
Norman Shumway

13. *Great teachers—"My teachers"*
   (1) *Bossier City, Louisiana*
        Olivett Montgomery
        Clayton Cornish

      Miss Stacey

(2) *Louisiana College*

      E. O. Wood

      V. B. Temple

      Richard Hawthorne

      Edgar Godbold

      Miss Hattie Strother

      H. H. Hobbs

(3) *Southern Seminary*

      Wayne Oates

      Clyde Francisco

      J. B. Weatherspoon

      V. L. Stanfield

      O. T. Binkley

(4) *Southwestern Seminary*

      Stewart A. Newman

      Earl Guinn

      R. T. Daniel

      Ray Summers

      T. B. Maston

      Ralph Smith

      Robert A. Baker

      L. R. Elliott

14. *Great friends—too many to name—*
in Bossier City, Louisiana
Shreveport, Louisiana
Pineville and Alexandria, Louisiana;
Louisville, Shelbyville, Waddy, and Harrisonville,
    Kentucky
Fort Worth, Texas; and around the world!
I thank God each day for friends!

What do "great people" in these fourteen groups do for me? They inspire me by showing how thay had courage, wisdom, steadfastness, faith, and talent. They inspire me by showing to me other people who have suffered and yet have won! I thank God that there have been such people.

You can seek out from the past or present great people who can furnish you examples of moral, physical, and spiritual courage. These great people cannot *give* you courage. Not at all. John Fitzgerald Kennedy said that such people could not supply courage, but they could inspire one to want courage. *To get courage, President Kennedy said that each one had to look deep inside himself.*

Of this, there can be no question; however, you can learn from great people that you can find faith and courage for almost every type of situation. Couple personal courage with the qualities you admire in great people, and you can find the sure path upward to victory!

Of this I am sure!

Others have! So can you!

It helps to be steadfast.

By "steadfast" I mean stickability.

Coach Vince Lombardi—the late great coach of the Green Bay Packers—taught his men to pay such a high price in preparation that they could not afford to quit when the going got rough.

Coach Darrell Royal, among others, has taught his Texas Longhorns, "When the going gets tough, the tough get going!"

There is something magnificent to me about a person who will not roll over, whimper, and quit when faced with a problem! Any problem!

There is something superb about a man or a woman or a young person who will cry out in anger, frustration, hurt, bewilderment, and fear—and still attempt to cope with the issue at hand. History is full of examples of people who have done this. Friend, people do this every day!

What about those who quit? Well, we don't know too much about them unless we live with them or near them! We don't know much about these people unless we are part of this quitting tribe.

However, we are told much in history about people who copped out on life by doing dastardly deeds—

John Wilkes Booth,
    Lee Harvey Oswald,
      Benedict Arnold,
Quisling,
    Brutus,
      Aaron Burr,
Bruno Richard Hauptmann,
John Dillinger,
    Al Capone and his gang,
      Pretty Boy Floyd,
      and others!

But we know almost nothing about the great hosts of people who "play the quitter" most of the time. Really, it is just as well that we have such limited data on quitters because, like the plague, we might catch this attitude from close association.

How much better it is to have what my college president Dr. Edgar Godbold, called "bull-dogged-hang-on-tive-ness!" Now, there is a word for all seasons! It grabs you! It holds you! It inspires you! Would you agree? It makes me want to keep on keeping on. It makes me want to get up again, no matter how many times I get knocked down.

Abe Martin, former coach and present athletic director

at Texas Christian University, told me once that success in athletics could be summed up in one sentence: The winner is the guy who gets up one more time than his opponent.

I like that!

Bill Russell, whom I consider to be not only the greatest basketball player in history but also the greatest athlete ever produced in America, told me that the "Celtic mystique" was the total dedication of each man to winning the game at hand. He said, "We never gave up. We might be 30 points behind with two minutes to play, but we never gave up." He said, "You see, all those other guys might fall down dead, and we could still win!" They never planned to quit! They never gave up! They lost some games, of course. Even the old Celtics lost a few. But, remember, they never gave up!

It is no wonder that Bill Russell and Red Auerbach led the Boston Celtics to eleven world championships in thirteen years.

Friend, it helps to follow the example of great people!

Friend, that's it! Ten things which you can believe and do. I hope that you have found something here which will uplift your heart.

I walked toward my fear!

You can walk toward yours!